—Leading businessmen, prominent politicians, and members of the Mafia have allied themselves in an unholy reign of terror.

—Naked violence and all-encompassing corruption have become a way of easy life for this elite of evil.

—Police look the other way at murder and judges let killers off with a gentle rap on their knuckles.

—A drug traffic flourishes that makes New York City look as clean as Disneyland.

—The death of Don Bolles was almost buried by official indifference and obfuscation until aroused public opinion and a team of crusaders lifted the lid off the whole bubbling scandal.

It can't happen here. You may say that about where you live. It was certainly what citizens of Arizona used to say about their beautiful, sun-drenched state. They think differently now. After reading this eye-opening Arizona exposé, so may you. Because what happened in Arizona can happen anywhere in the U.S.A.

Don Bolles

An Investigation into His Murder

by Martin Tallberg

POPULAR LIBRARY • NEW YORK

Published by Popular Library, a unit of CBS
Publications, the Consumer Publishing Division
of CBS Inc.

December, 1977

Copyright © 1977 by Martin Tallberg

ISBN: 0-445-04122-6

*I'd like to dedicate this book to two Dons,
one fictional and one factual.*

Don Quixote
&
Don Bolles

*Thank God for men who find it necessary
to charge at windmills!*

Martin Tallberg

CONTENTS

Chapter 1

A DAY IN JUNE

JUNE 2, 1976

Phoenix, Arizona. It's 11:35 A.M. In a parking lot adjacent to the Clarendon, a small midtown hotel, Don Bolles, a tall, bespectacled reporter for the *Arizona Republic*, saunters up to his parked car. He stands for a moment, contemplating perhaps some minor frustration or merely reminiscing on this his eighth wedding anniversary. Then he opens the car door and eases his six-foot-two-inch frame into the little white Datsun. Placing his reporter's notebook on the seat beside him, he shuts the door and casually inserts his key in the ignition switch. An unhurried man, Bolles sits for another moment, turning over in his mind the series of events that has brought him to this parking lot, on this day, at this time. Though the scheduled appointment at the hotel fell through, there's the Sigma Delta Chi luncheon at noon, some legislative stuff to check on this afternoon, and let's see . . . Oh yes! he's taking Rosalie to the movies tonight. "I wonder," he muses, "if *All the President's Men* is anywhere near an accurate reflection of investigative reporting."

Finally, he tromps on the clutch pedal, gives the ignition key a twist, and the small Japanese engine springs to life. As it settles into a confident idle, the reporter looks around to see if the driveway is clear. There's no one in sight. So his practiced hand shifts the gear selector to reverse, his left foot eases off the clutch pedal, and Don Bolles slowly starts to back from his parking space.

Nearby, a pudgy finger creeps slowly toward a push button mounted on a small black metal box. It pauses for a moment, as if searching for the proper place to touch, then settles carefully on the button . . . and pushes.

Suddenly the little white Datsun in the parking lot leaps in the air, erupting smoke and flame. The booming crack of exploding dynamite is heard. The concussion slams into the hotel, smashing windows and spraying shrapnel. The car door bursts open . . . and the reporter is hurled from the vehicle to sprawl grotesquely on the pavement. Glasses shattered, clothing shredded, Bolles lies gasping on the macadam, his torso face down and his mangled legs still partially entrapped in the wrecked and smoking car.

"Oh, my God! What was that?" is a simultaneous reaction throughout the relatively quiet neighborhood. Among the startled is Lonnie Reed, an air-conditioning repairman installing an exhaust fan across the street. Another is Ann Neroda, a computer programmer walking through a nearby parking lot on her way to lunch. A third is Mrs. Lois Damashek, a retired Army nurse who's reading a newsmagazine in a nearby apartment. Stunned for an instant by the shocking sound of the blast, their recovery is swift.

Reed drops his tools and rushes across the street to the Clarendon parking lot. As he nears the smoking car, he sees the reporter lying in an expanding pool of blood, and hears his heart-wrenching pleas, "Help me! Help me!" Reed, once a surgical orderly, notes the flow of blood and reacts with a remembered professional instinct. He quickly strips the belt from his Levis and fastens it around one of Bolles' mutilated legs.

Ann Neroda rushes up and takes a look. One glance

is enough. With horror written on her face, she turns and sprints back across the street to the bank where she works to call an ambulance.

Lois Damashek, the former Army nurse, tells in her own words what happened: "I was sitting in my apartment with the Arcadia door open, reading one of the weekly newsmagazines. I thought the explosion was in our building because I had reported the smell of gas in the laundry room on a couple of occasions. So I jumped out on the balcony, and I saw the manager's wife come out who lives right above the laundry, and I said, 'Was that in our building?' She said, 'No, it was at the Clarendon!' Of course, then I could see the smoke, and you could still hear the glass breaking, and I could hear a woman screaming. I thought it was a kitchen explosion at the Clarendon. That's when I ran. I just grabbed some dressings and started over in the direction of the smoke. Lonnie Reed was putting on a second tourniquet when I arrived. I have timed myself since the bombing, doing exactly what happened, retracing with a digital watch. So I was there within two minutes and some seconds after it occurred. There were such terrible . . . terrible wounds! He was bleeding arterially and veinously, there was no flesh on the back of his legs. On the entire surface there was an extravasation of blood, and we couldn't see, but I expected that there were wounds in the lower abdomen and groin. The way he was plopped out of that car! The torso was face down, and his legs were still up in the car, and we couldn't even see if the leg was severed. However, there was bleeding from the lower part of the leg . . . pulsating bleeding. We didn't dare move him, all we tried to do was keep him from going into shock. He could talk! Then someone was kneeling over him sort of pushing his head down. She was trying to prevent him from seeing his injuries. I said, 'Don't push his head down, it embarrasses respiration!' But he sort of raised up on his arms . . . and turned to see."

Through a fogging consciousness, reporter Don Bolles stares at what is left of his legs, and in bewildered agony mutters, "Son of a bitch!"

Mrs. Damashek continues, "There's a kind of blindness that hits you when you see something like this. In thirty years of nursing, I have not been able to get over the emotional feeling that you get when you see a badly injured animal or human being . . . when you see flesh destroyed like this . . . especially when they are conscious. It's a very terrible thing!"

The crowd in the parking lot continues to gather. Most stay at a respectful distance, fearful of another explosion. Over the mutterings of excited conversation, sirens and the whoop-whoop sounds of emergency vehicles are heard. Engine Nine and a ladder truck from the Phoenix Fire Department roar around the corner and pull up to the parking lot. Before the vehicles have come to a halt, the blue-shirted fire fighters are off and running. Some head for the blasted car, others with practiced motion grab first-aid kits and other emergency supplies. The crowd gives way to let the firemen through. It's a typical scene of orderly chaos.

Kneeling around the still conscious reporter, the firemen check the first aid already administered. One attempts to solicit a medical history from the downed newsman. Another rushes up with an oxygen canister and mask. In a strained and rapidly weakening voice, Bolles tries to answer the questions and pass on information that his still lucid mind believes important. "Telephone my wife!" he gasps. "They finally got me! . . . The Mafia . . . Emprise . . . Find John Adamson!" These are his final words as the oxygen mask is placed over his face.

The ambulance arrives and the decision is made to transport immediately. Paramedics from Rescue Six are on their way, but the blood loss is all too evident . . . and as the minicam units from KOOL-TV record the scene for posterity, the firemen lift Bolles onto a gurney and slide him into the metal womb of the emergency vehicle.

In the newsroom of the *Arizona Republic*, a place resembling an Eagle's Hall filled with rows of desks and clacking typewriters, the tension is mounting. It has been learned that an investigative reporter has been "hit." It isn't the expected prime target, Al Sitter, a *Republic* reporter often threatened for his revelations in print. Al has just walked in. "Who in the hell could it be?" As this question permeates the newsroom's somewhat smoky atmosphere, a telephone rings on the desk of City Editor Bob Early. He grabs at the instrument, identifies himself, and listens. In a moment he blanches and mutters, "Jesus Christ!" He mutters a few more words into the phone, then with slow deliberation places it back on its cradle. "It's Bolles!" As these softly spoken words reverberate from mouth to ear around the room, Early questions himself and those around him, "What the hell was he working on?" No one answers. Slowly City Editor Early gets up from his chair, walks over to reporter Dave Spriggs, puts a hand on his shoulder, and says, "He's at St. Joseph's Hospital." No other word is necessary as Spriggs dashes for the elevator. Then, in a louder voice, cracking with emotion, Early announces to the rest of the city room, "Nobody leaves!" This order isn't necessary, as any lunchtime hunger pangs have long since been drowned in a welling flood of sadness, frustration, and visceral wrath.

As returning professionalism pierces the shock of the moment, columnist Paul Dean, best man at Don Bolles' wedding eight years ago, marches purposefully toward Early's desk and demands assignment to the story. The

11

city editor looks up at Dean's grim-visaged face and nods his assent.

While Dean grabs his notebook and runs for the elevator, Early begins issuing orders and assignments. The gears of purposeful journalism start to mesh, and the biggest personal story to hit the Phoenix newspaper gathers momentum. Actually it's far more than a story, for deep within every newsman on the staff there's a personal and desperate need to do *something*, and since a journalist's work is the gathering of information, at the *Arizona Republic* this work begins . . . with a passion!

JUNE 2, 1976

Phoenix, Arizona. It's 6:30 P.M. In the corridors and waiting room of St. Joseph's Hospital, the contingent of friends, relatives, blood donors, police officers, and members of the news-gathering media mill nervously, awaiting some word on the condition of reporter Don Bolles. He's been in the operating room for over five hours. Rumors are rampant, and whispered speculation helps pass the time. It's known that Don still lives. It's known that he's seriously injured. But the extent of his injuries and his chances for life remain unknown. Finally a hospital spokesman makes an appearance where the anxious are gathered. "I have an announcement," he says. Television camera lights snap on, tape recorder buttons are pushed, and reporters' notebooks are opened. A hush comes over the group as Bolles' condition is described in the sterile adjectives of medical terminology. His right leg has been amputated above the knee, and for hours a team of surgeons has been picking bomb fragments and shrapnel from other parts of his body. Though he is alive, Don Bolles' condition is listed as critical.

At the *Republic* and *Gazette* building, six hours

have passed. The afternoon paper, the *Phoenix Gazette*, has managed to remake page one and include some short stories on the bombing in its Home and Green Sheet editions. Though both the *Republic* and *Gazette* have the same ownership, they have separate and somewhat rival staffs.

In the *Republic* city room, Paul Dean has returned from the scene of the explosion and is putting the finishing touches to his page-one feature story.

"Was it a warning?" he writes. "Was it vengeance to equal the score of an old exposé? Was it a direct threat to scare other newsmen from poking into land frauds, gambling monopolies, business scams, or organized crime?"

These questions ending Dean's first story on the Bolles bombing were on the lips of every newsman in the state.

At another desk, Earl Zarbin is working on the lead story. He and Jack West have been assigned. West, an outstanding police reporter, is the outside man, gathering the latest facts on the police investigation and periodically telephoning what he has learned back to Zarbin, the inside man.

As he waits for West's periodic reports, Earl is busy trying to check out other facets of the story by making his own phone calls, while also attempting to piece the various bits of information in to some form of a coherent story. In the charged, hyperactive atmosphere of the city room coherence is not easily achieved.

As Zarbin's practiced fingers punch the typewriter keys, portions of the lead story begin to take shape. From Jack West, he learns that the police are now certain that Bolles was deliberately lured to the Clarendon to set him up for the assassination attempt. Detective Dan Dryden told West and other reporters that the bomb was placed underneath the floor on the driver's side, below the forward edge of the seat.

13

"It was placed in such a manner as to kill—not to warn," Dryden said.

The Phoenix detective volunteered some other details. He said that Don had backed his car a little over one car length and cocked the wheels to the right, and was getting ready to drive out of the parking lot when the blast occurred.

Zarbin writes, "Bolles, in his years as a *Republic* reporter investigating organized crime and political and white collar corruption, had received many threats on his life. But this was the first time an attempt actually had been made to kill him."

On the other side of the *Republic* city room, reporter Tom Kuhn is doing a reaction piece. He has contacted top state officials for their immediate personal reaction, and all have expressed anger and outrage.

State Attorney General Bruce Babbitt calls the bombing attack "an incredibly brazen attempt to intimidate everybody working on the problem of organized crime and corruption."

Governor Raul Castro offers $1,000 to add to the $25,000 offered by the *Republic* and *Gazette* as a reward for information leading to the arrest and conviction of those responsible for the attack, and expresses the hope that everyone will be galvanized into taking proper, responsible action in the battle against crime.

The Arizona Senate in a statement signed by both Republican and Democrat leaders pledges "the fullest resources of our state in bringing justice to the persons responsible for this cowardly attack."

Mayor Margaret Hance breaks into tears when informed of the Bolles bombing, and says Phoenix will not become the kind of city in which such occurrences are commonplace.

Vernon Hoy, DPS director, and Roger Young of the FBI pledge their assistance, as well as countless others.

Reporter Connie Koenenn meanwhile is digging into the files to answer Bob Early's question, "What was he working on?"

When she finally sits down at the typewriter, her first paragraph reads, "Investigative reporter Don Bolles has written exposés by the score for the *Arizona Republic*, accelerating the pace in the late 1960s. In some of them may lie the clue to the attempt to assassinate him Wednesday with a bomb."

Connie continues, and tells of Bolles' warnings that organized crime was moving into Arizona, that land developments, gambling, and restaurants were attracting mobsters to the area from Las Vegas, Chicago, and Detroit.

She also tells of Bolles' series of articles in 1967 which dug into Western Growth Capital Corporation and was the *Republic*'s first major effort in an exposé of land fraud in the state. It was a series, she wrote, that told in detail of a scheme in which over a thousand persons were ripped off, people who had bought land, stock, or notes in Western Growth Capital before it went under.

As Connie's fingers flit with purpose across the keyboard, more on Bolles' investigations unfolds.

How Don revealed promoter Ned Warren's participation in the land fraud operation, and the corporate structures that were set up to make it possible, and how Bolles dug up facts on Warren's previous criminal record—these appear on the paper in Connie's machine. It continues, and explains that despite many stories on Warren and his associates by Bolles and others, there appeared to be little official concern with land fraud until 1975, when a Phoenix accountant, Edward Lazar, was murdered just one day before he was scheduled to testify before a Maricopa County grand jury on Warren's activities. It was then that Don Bolles was finally able to write, "Spurred by the gangland-style slaying of a grand jury land fraud witness last week, Arizona lawmakers are trying to fashion new tools against land crooks."

When it was finished, Connie's article had revealed a number of Bolles' investigatory exposures.

In addition to the articles on land fraud and Ned Warren, Bolles had focused his attention through the years on a sports concession operation which was part of a Buffalo, New York, corporate structure then known as the Emprise Corporation. Bolles and Congressman Sam Steiger suspicioned that Emprise was mob-connected, and through loans and pressure was slowly taking control of all the horse and dog racing tracks in Arizona.

In 1973 Bolles and Jack West wrote a series entitled "The Newcomers," in which it was said that a number of nationally known reputed mob figures had been spotted by law-enforcement officers in Phoenix restaurants.

These alleged mobsters included:

—William Kaiser of Joliet, Illinois, a reputed associate of Chicago syndicate hoodlums, according to state police, and a former operator of a vending-machine route in that city.

—Joseph P. English, a brother of deceased "Fat Sam" English, who had been labeled as a member of the Chicago syndicate by the McClellan Committee and the Chicago Crime Commission.

—Charles C. Verive, who had been one of the persons indicted in a million-dollar Chicago fraud case, and was called by authorities a former muscleman.

Bolles at the time wrote, "Police agencies admit they are hard pressed to keep up with the surging influx into Arizona of individuals known to be relatives or close associates of notorious figures in organized crime."

What Connie Koenenn inadvertently omitted from her story was Don's more recent revelations at the state

16

Legislature and his stories which caused embarrassment to Governor Castro and his appointee to the state Racing Commission, Kemper Marley.

Back at Zarbin's desk, the lead story was falling into place. It detailed the events leading up to the bombing. Bolles, it said, received a phone call last week from a man who alleged he had information on a land deal involving Senator Barry Goldwater, Congressman Sam Steiger, and Harry Rosenzweig, former GOP state chairman and lifelong friend of Senator Goldwater's.

Bolles said that according to the informant some money had exchanged hands and he also knew about some other stuff on Steiger that he would reveal, and according to a colleague, Bernie Wynn, political columnist for the *Arizona Republic*, Bolles arranged to meet the informant either that day or the next. Wynn said that Bolles went out to meet him, and after talking with the informant was not impressed. He told Wynn that the man was a "sleazy bastard," supposedly from San Diego. During the meeting the "sleazy" informant promised to give Bolles more information and documentation, and promised to bring another person with information.

"That's all there was until yesterday [Tuesday], when Don said the guy called and was ready for another meeting, and that he was going to meet with him today," Wynn recalled.

"So, Don left me a note [Wednesday, June 2] in my typewriter. He left here [Senate press room] about eleven o'clock. The note said: 'I've gone to meet that guy with the information on Steiger at the Clarendon House. Then to Sigma Delta Chi. Back about 1:30 P.M. Bolles.' "

It was also disclosed that later in the afternoon some colleagues who occupied the Senate press room with Don Bolles found a note in Bolles' handwriting that said, "John Adamson . . . Lobby at 11:15 . . . Clarendon House . . . 4th & Clarendon."

"Who in the hell is John Adamson?" everyone asked.

JUNE 3, 1976

In a hospital room at St. Joseph's, two Phoenix policemen stand at the bedside of bombed reporter Don Bolles. Breathing tubes are supplying supplemental oxygen to the injured man's lungs, and he is unable to speak. Though listed as "critical" he is alert and lucid, responding to yes and no questions from the officers.

"Is this the man you were scheduled to meet?" Bolles responds affirmatively with a nod of the head as he is shown a photograph. "Is this the man you know to be John Adamson?" Again Bolles nods his affirmation.

JUNE 4, 1976

8 A.M. The *Arizona Republic* has been on the stands for several hours, saying in its headline story:

Don Bolles identified from his hospital bed Thursday a photograph of the man who lured him to the hotel where the *Arizona Republic* reporter was critically injured in a bomb blast on Wednesday.

Bolles, though in extremely critical condition at St. Joseph's Hospital, identified a picture of John Harvey Adamson, 33. Adamson is a known acquaintance of Ned Warren, Sr., the so-called godfather of Arizona land-fraud schemes.

Police are searching for Adamson.

Phoenix Police lieutenant Jack Bentley said Adamson is the "key to the investigation."

18

Through the doors of the Phoenix Police Department building two men enter. One is a nattily attired young attorney, Stephan Scott, the second is a moon-faced individual, with metal frame sunglasses, 6 feet 1 inch, 214 pounds, wearing a white leisure suit. He is identified to officers as John Harvey Adamson.

In moments Scott and Adamson are rushed upstairs to the Criminal Investigation Division. There waiting are Police Captain Don Lozier, detectives Dan Dryden and Jon Sellers, and other members of the criminal investigation bureau. Adamson and Scott are ushered into an interrogation room and seated. A stenographer is called in, and one of the detectives begins reciting the words from his "Miranda" card. "You have the right to remain silent. Anything you say can be used against you in a court of law. You have a right to the presence of an attorney to assist you prior to questioning, and to be with you during questioning, if you so desire. If you cannot afford an attorney, you have the right to have an attorney appointed for you prior to questioning. Do you understand these rights?" Adamson nods. "And will you voluntarily answer my questions?"

Adamson sits mute, saying nothing, not even his name.

Attorney Scott explains that Adamson will not respond to police questioning at this time.

After some consultation and discussion, Adamson is informed that he must accompany detectives Dryden and Sellers to the Maricopa County Jail, where he will be booked on an outstanding charge against him, a misdemeanor complaint of defrauding an innkeeper.

At ten forty-eight that morning Adamson is freed on a $100 bond.

Questioned that day by newsmen, Police Captain Don Lozier says, "We don't have sufficient probable cause to bring any kind of charge [relating to Bolles' bombing] against Mr. Adamson at this time. That doesn't mean that we might not develop other information."

Some newsmen quiz Lozier on whether Adamson can be held for a time without a charge. "No!" is the captain's response. "An old law permitting such detention for seventy-two hours has been changed."

As Adamson leaves the county jail after less than three hours in custody, there is no apparent surveillance by police officers. But he is confronted by a mini-host of reporters and photographers who have been assigned to dog his footsteps. Using three cars and lots of shoe leather, they tail the irritated Adamson throughout the city despite his attempts to elude them.

Next morning's *Arizona Republic* details his movements:

> At First Avenue and Madison they [Adamson and attorney Scott] were picked up by Scott's secretary, who drove them back to the police building, where Scott and Adamson re-entered Scott's auto and drove to his office.
>
> Scott had said that he wanted a quiet place in which to talk to Adamson and they remained at his office until shortly after noon, when they went to the Under 3 at 3 W. Monroe for lunch.
>
> After lunch, Scott drove Adamson to the First Federal Building at 3003 N. Central. Adamson went to the office of attorney Tom Foster, leaving there about 4 P.M. and walking north a few doors to the Ivanhoe Cocktail Lounge, 3033 N. Central.
>
> Adamson spent the remainder of the afternoon and early evening there, except for about 30 minutes during which he got a manicure at the Continental Hair Styling salon, 3003 N. Central.
>
> He returned at 5:40 P.M. [to the Ivanhoe

20

Lounge], ordered another straight cranberry juice on the rocks, and joined the secretaries and businessmen at the bar.

At 6:15 P.M., a long-distance telephone call came to the bar for Adamson. It was from Canada.

"Hi, Doctor," said Adamson.

The conversation covered salmon fishing, an inquiry about a woman called Mary, and soft talk drowned by talk around the bar.

While in the Ivanhoe, Adamson's shoes were taken out to be shined.

. . . and so the media watch of John Harvey Adamson continued.

JUNE 5, 1976

At St. Joseph's Hospital, a spokesman announces that Don Bolles underwent a tracheotomy to relieve throat soreness caused by tubes attached to his breathing apparatus. The spokesman elaborates on the reporter's condition. "Although blood continued to seep from his wounds, his vital signs were good. He is responding to kidney dialysis treatment and seems to be gaining strength, but he's still in critical condition."

Meanwhile, detective Mike Grant is meeting with Bolles' wife, Rosalie, at the hospital. He tells reporters later in the day, "She said she had been very concerned for his safety when he was working as an investigative reporter. She also said that since he has been covering the state Legislature, he has been so very busy that he has been avoiding making appointments; an appointment concerning anything else would have had to be very important to him." Grant adds, "She called us because she thought we should know what she could tell us. One thing, she's a lady with a lot of guts."

21

It's also revealed that Arizona governor Raul Castro visited with Mrs. Bolles at the hospital yesterday.

JUNE 8, 1976

At St. Joseph's Hospital, Don Bolles' condition is worsening.

Paul Dean and Jack West, reporting the story in the *Arizona Republic*, say, "Doctors described Bolles' condition as very grave."

The *Republic* story also indicates progress in the investigation. "Phoenix detectives say they have developed 'three or four possible motives' in the bombing. Capt. Don Lozier said that at least one motive involves 'big-name political figures,' but added that John Harvey Adamson, 32, of 4650 N. 11th Ave., remains a 'focal point of the investigation.'"

Events, however, are taking place more rapidly than the print media's ability to communicate their happening. Even as Phoenicians drink their orange juice and read the morning paper, doctors are preparing to amputate Don Bolles' right arm.

At 10:40 A.M., Don Bolles emerges from the operating room as a double amputee.

JUNE 9, 1976

Bolles' condition is stabilizing somewhat.

JUNE 10, 1976

Bolles worsens. With infection setting in to the reporter's remaining leg, his groin, and lower torso, another tough medical decision is made.

Bolles emerges from the operating room as a triple amputee.

JUNE 12, 1976

Doctors express guarded optimism on his chances for survival, though Bolles remains in critical condition.

JUNE 13, 1976

It's Sunday. Some Arizonans are entering church for the eleven o'clock service. Others are out on the golf course. Most are just lazing around the house. It's a typical Sunday, seemingly designed for contemplation and relaxation.

At St. Joseph's Hospital, grim-faced members of the news media file in to a hastily called news conference. A weary, obviously depressed Dr. William Dozer, Don Bolles' personal physician, winds his way through the crowd and takes his position as a focus of attention. In the quiet of a hush, he clears his throat, and announces the terrible but expected news. "Don Bolles is dead."

As tears come to the eyes of hard-nosed reporters, Dozer continues, "He put up the most courageous fight I have ever seen any person put up for his life."

The details of his death follow. "A couple of days ago, I was optimistic about his recovery, but Bolles' condition for about twelve to twenty hours before his death was characterized by 'mild deterioration' leading to the sudden lung complications that ended his life. Bolles' wife, Rosalie, was at his bedside when he died."

At 1:30 P.M., two and a half hours after Bolles' death, the Phoenix police picked up John Harvey Adamson on a charge of murder.

Chapter 2

OUTRAGE IN ARIZONA

Bolles dead!

Never in the history of the state has the death of a single individual Arizonan had such an impact.

While the bombing had generated a plethora of anger and concern, Bolles' actual death gave the vicious act its terrible dimension. For eleven painful days he had courageously battled the inevitable, and the public responded. There was a general feeling in the state that even in his fight for life Don Bolles was giving Arizona an example to follow, that every gasping breath he took was demonstrating the courageous attitude necessary to combat the state's existing evils.

Death, it was felt, was not the just trophy for this champion.

The feelings of the moment were well expressed by publisher Nina Pulliam in a front-page box of the Monday, June 14, edition of the *Arizona Republic:*

> Don Bolles is dead. He has given the last full measure of devotion for those high principles on which he stood and fought so courageously and so effectively in his relentless war on crime in this community.
>
> Don Bolles is gone, but the fearless, tenacious spirit which motivated and sustained him in his

work—and in his heroic but losing battle for life—will live on.

The *Arizona Republic* and the *Phoenix Gazette* do not intend that Don Bolles' death shall go unavenged. Even deeper than our profound grief are our anger and our outrage at the monstrous violation of all human rights and decency responsible for it. We will leave no leaf unturned in our commitment to see justice done in this terrible tragedy.

We call on every element of our society to join us now in the continuing fight—in Don Bolles' life-long fight—to wipe out for all time the criminal elements which debase and terrify this community.

We could not rest if Don Bolles had died utterly in vain.

Governor Raul Castro ordered flags to half-mast throughout Arizona.

In Washington, President Ford said he was distressed and outraged that a reporter in search of truth became an apparent victim of the underworld.

U. S. Senator Barry Goldwater of Arizona gave this personal comment: "I've known Don as long as he has been here. He was a very fine man, a decent man.

"It's all right if those things happen to an SOB, but not to a guy like this," Goldwater snarled.

"We have had several things like this happen out here," he interjected, "but we've sort of laughed it off, saying, 'Well, it happened here but it was an accident.'

"There's always been the feeling that Arizona was sort of a place of peace, but we can't feel that way now," Goldwater emphasized.

Phoenix Mayor Margaret Hance, moved by Bolles' struggle to live, said, "Don's fight for life was an inspiration to all of us. He lost his fight, but I pray that we will not forget him or what he was trying to do—create a decent, safe environment for all the citizens of Arizona."

State Senate President Bob Stump (now a congressman) said he was checking to see what could be done about legislation on white collar crime.

State House Majority Leader Burton Barr said, "We can't let this incident be forgotten."

And so the reaction went.

Most of the public anger and outrage that followed the announcement of Bolles' death reminded one of the feelings expressed immediately after Pearl Harbor and the assassination of President Kennedy.

Some reaction, however, was a bit more cynical (or realistic).

"What's the use?" said Frank Novak, a Phoenix citizen. "After the cops catch him [the perpetrator of the bombing], the judge'll give him a plea bargain and he'll get five to ten years."

Another said, "It's a hell of a thing! It's terrible that it would happen to anyone, especially to someone who reports the news. We should stop it [organized crime] if we can. But can we? That's a great question!"

As a news story, the murder of Don Bolles was front page. Throughout the world this killing was seen as something special. Even in the Soviet Union, a news periodical featured a story on Don Bolles and Arizona.

Why?

Why should the death of one investigative news reporter create such a stir?

The answer, perhaps, is that in a free society with a free press, the investigative reporter is given the awesome task of being a surrogate conscience for the community he serves.

Robert Greene, Pulitzer Prize winner, and the head of a reporters' group investigating crime in the state since Bolles' death, concurs: "Bolles was killed because of what he was doing, and what he was doing [investigating crime and corruption] we more or less universally accept as right. In the American ethic, we are supposed to fight crime, we are supposed to fight corruption."

Another factor which may have helped generate such worldwide interest in the Bolles murder was a fear that new and brutal rules were being initiated into the game of American business and politics. Had intimidation of the free press been added to the bribery, lying, and cheating of the Watergate era? Whatever the reason, the murder of Don Bolles was deemed news of worldwide importance.

Probably the very first significant bit of information learned in a high school journalism class is the value of the five W's and the H in reporting a story, that is, *who, what, why, where, when,* and *how.*

These are the essential ingredients to a complete news story, and Don Bolles knew them well.

So, in following these precepts of good journalism, we ask the question, just "who" was Don Bolles?

His biographical data show that he was born July 10, 1928, in Milwaukee. His father, Donald F. Bolles, Sr., was a reporter and later a bureau chief for the Associated Press. Apparently Don's proclivity for journalism was the result of genetics, conditioning, and filial respect, for as he often told colleagues, "Even as a youngster, I always wanted to be a reporter."

He graduated from Teaneck High School in Teaneck, New Jersey, and then attended Beloit College in Wisconsin. He graduated from Beloit in 1950 and joined the Army for the Korean "police action." Assigned to an anti-aircraft battery, Bolles attained the rank of first lieutenant. In 1953, after discharge from the service, Bolles joined the Associated Press. He worked as a rewrite man and sports editor for AP until

1962, when he joined the staff of the *Arizona Republic* in Phoenix.

Initially assigned to cover the state Capitol and the Arizona Supreme Court, Bolles quickly impressed the *Republic*'s editorial management with his ability to dig below the surface and unearth factual stories and information.

In 1965, he was nominated for a Pulitzer prize for his series of investigative stories involving bribery, kickbacks, and other irregularities in the Arizona Tax Commission and the state Corporation Commission. These stories led to the indictment of two tax commissioners and the impeachment of two corporation commissioners. Though the charges were dismissed, the politicians involved either did not seek re-election or were defeated at the polls.

In 1967, Bolles spearheaded the newspaper's first major effort to expose land fraud in Arizona. His articles revealed the inner workings of the various corporations which had been set up to peddle land, sell mortgages, and handle utilities.

This series concentrated on Western Growth Capital Corporation, a firm which was sold by land promoter Ned Warren, Sr., to Lee Ackerman, businessman and unsuccessful candidate for governor. The company folded shortly after the sale, and Ackerman sued Warren for $40 million. Court officers said that "questionable" sales practices had undercut the finances of the company. This bankruptcy caused thousands of trusting investors to lose their money.

Bolles' articles revealed how salesmen were peddling land for 5 per cent down, then would split a 20 per cent commission with the buyer, who would promptly default. They also revealed that Ned Warren had served time at Sing Sing and the federal correctional institution at Danbury, Connecticut, before he came to

Arizona in 1961, and connected the names of respected Arizona businessmen with the land-scam operation.

It was just a beginning!

Arizona has, in certain quarters, the reputation of being a rather conservative Western state with God-fearing politicians and "the kind of folks you can trust." Yet, scrape away the desert patina and you'll find in its two major cities, Phoenix and Tucson, some of the worst crime statistics in the nation. It has a statewide drug-traffic problem that makes old New York seem a paragon of virtue, a political and legal establishment that would warm the cockles of Al Capone's heart, and of course, land frauds which seem to have been concocted by the collective efforts of Niccolò Machiavelli and Carlo Ponzi. Authorities estimate over $500 million has been lost in land-related swindles over the past ten years.

The *New York Times* in an article on June 14, one day after the Bolles' death, said, "Under the gaze of a sweltering desert sun, a hybrid breed of organized crime—including Mafia-style emigres from elsewhere and a home-grown species of seemingly respectable business and professional men—is blossoming in Arizona, the nation's fastest-growing state.

"Largely through vast fraudulent land deals, securities frauds, and other, often related 'white collar crimes,' criminal groups are turning over many millions of dollars a year in illicit profits, bringing gangland-style violence to this fast urbanizing frontier state and provoking unresolved charges of official corruption."

A key phrase in the *Times* article, and perhaps the key to a real understanding of the problems facing this Southwestern section of the nation, is "the nation's fastest-growing state."

In 1940, the population of Arizona was a mere 499,000. By 1976, it had reached an estimated 2,345,000, three quarters of whom live in the Phoenix and Tucson areas. Phoenix alone has over a million. The real dollar values of the manufacturing industry in Arizona has grown from 654 million in 1964 to 2,270 million in 1974. That's an increase of 246 per cent . . . in ten years!

The *Times* article quotes Kevin O'Malley, a lawyer for the Justice Department's Crime Strike Force, as saying, "There's a great deal of money in Arizona, and when you have a great deal of money you have a fertile field for organized crime."

The term "organized crime" often conjures up images of *The Godfather* or an old James Cagney movie. Such is not the case!

While some residue of the old "garlic Mafia" remains, the old blood ties and family structures have been largely dissipated in the realities of "computer age" money-making. Trite but true, among criminals or the righteous, money is still the name of the game.

Don Bolles expressed it well in a rather ironical statement while addressing a women's club in 1971:

"No longer are criminals coming into a community recognized by their resemblance to the movie stereotypes of the thirties, and, in general, do not use the same methods of those days. Crime does not pay if bodies are left all over the street, since it arouses public notice to an extent that quiet penetration of business does not."

Irony indeed, since one of Don Bolles' last spoken words was "Mafia."

It *is* difficult, however, to determine the location and the extent to which legitimate business has been penetrated by money from criminal sources.

Aided and abetted by greedy lawyers, modern crime syndicates have learned that it is often more profitable to use the law than break it.

Arizona State University professor James Johnson, a sociologist interested in criminality in the business world, and land fraud in particular, says, "a corporation is an ideal shield for land crooks.

"It's the key instrument used by organized crime," Professor Johnson contends. In reference to corporate thievery, he points out, "A corporation can go bankrupt and leave the owners and officers financially untouched. While a corporate veil protects the owners' personal assets, a bankruptcy leaves the victims struggling with each other for the remaining fragments of the corporation.

"To sue the owners of corporations successfully," Johnson explains, "land fraud victims must prove that the owners, directors, and officers conspired to defraud them. Without proving conspiracy, the underlings will be blamed for the corporation's failure and the owners will be untouchable."

According to reliable sources, no corporation has ever gone to jail!

Professor Johnson comments further, "The public tends to think of corporations in terms of IBM or General Motors. But, in reality the corporations that are often involved in land sales are shells, incorporated for an annual cost of $42 in Arizona and practically unregulated."

In practical terms, this means that corporations are devices whereby a group of persons can transact business without putting their personal finances in jeopardy. It also means that crooks of various ilk and feather can put together a bilking business, suck hard-earned money from customers or investors, then let the business fold after this money has been transferred to their personal treasuries.

Arizona Corporation Commissioner Ernest Garfield explains, "As far as corporations in this state are concerned, if they do not sell securities or they are not a utility, they are totally unregulated. Because all they are required to do is submit certain forms according to law, and then we *must* approve them. We have no discretion at all!"

Barry Aarons, director of Arizona's Incorporating Division, amplifies, "Most states have even less filing requirements than we have. Most states operate corporate licensing the same way you would license your automobile. That is, you come, and you send a little postcard later saying, I'm still in business, and here's my five, ten, hundred dollars, whatever it costs, and you continue to operate. Very little information is required. States like New Jersey, Illinois, California, their corporate annual report is just that type of postcard saying, Hey! I'm still in business, and here's my filing fee."

Many corporations, of course, are legitimate purposeful concerns which do credit to the concept of private enterprise. The problem, however, is the inability to sift the wheat from the chaff. In Arizona and most other states, there is no requirement to verify the identity of persons who establish or operate corporations. Names listed on corporate records may be real, aliases, or completely fictitious.

As to a criminal check of corporate names, Barry Aarons says, "There is no state that currently runs a criminal check."

Certain businesses such as banks, liquor establishments, racetracks, utilities, and companies who sell stock and securities are regulated to varying degrees by the various states. Real estate is also regulated to a degree, depending upon the laws of the individual state. But the amount of regulation is directly dependent upon the amount of enforcement applied. In recent years, the facilities needed and the desire to enforce the regulations on the books have been minimal in the state of Arizona. Laws and regulations are only words printed on pieces of paper unless they are enforced, and the current unsavory reputation of the state is partially due to a lack of enforcement.

Licensing and criminal checks are required for a number of persons employed by or functioning as management for regulated corporations. As to the ownership of such corporations, the requirements are quite different.

To receive the benefits of a corporate status, as was mentioned earlier, there is little information required. A list of incorporators (officers and board members) and the statutory agent (usually a lawyer), the purpose of the corporation, and some other miscellaneous information are usually all that is demanded by state law. The requirements for financial data are sparse. Aarons relates:

"Five states currently require a balance sheet upon qualification. Eight states, and only eight states, require a financial statement on the annual report. Interestingly enough, one state recently has just added the requirement that a corporation file a copy of its Schedule L, from its federal income tax returns, as part of its annual report—and that's Delaware. Delaware is the king of corporate states. If you want to form a corporation you go to Delaware."

In recent years, since corporate activities and "white collar crime" have come to the public's attention, attempts to investigate the business community have been frustrated by an inordinate lack of information. Only in situations of gross and clearly evident violations of the law, in which law enforcement agencies can get a subpoena to look over state and federal income tax returns, have the police and other investigators been able to get behind the corporate façade. This inability to scrutinize the components of the corporate structure has permitted blatant organized criminals to take over legitimate businesses and launder their ill-gotten money through these pristine operations.

The major effect of criminal infiltration of business is to lower the moral and ethical standards of the entire business community. To survive, the legitimate businessman must begin to cut corners. In a free-market situation, unethical or criminal elements have a distinct advantage, and if the legitimate businessman is to remain competitive he must adopt the tactics and techniques of his unethical opponent. As one businessman begins to cut corners, it forces his competition to do the same or more, and this in turn creates a descending spiral in business ethics and morality.

In Arizona, the death of Don Bolles seemed to indicate a new low.

While most law enforcement investigators agree that current mobsters of organized crime prefer to use financial muscle rather than the crude strong-arm tactics of bygone years, the old Capone days rub-outs are by no means alien to Arizona.

In a June 13 article in the *Arizona Republic*, John Winters writes: "Eight times in the past two decades gangland figures have struck down Phoenix residents—and seven times they have gotten away with murder."

Winters chronicled the mob-style killings which began in April 1955 with the murder of Mrs. Charles Greenbaum. Mrs. Greenbaum was married to a brother of Gus Greenbaum, who had moved to Phoenix in 1928 and later established a "horse wire" and off-track gambling operation. Gus Greenbaum's bookie setup was technically illegal, but in the wide-open days of the 1930s and 1940s it was perfectly acceptable in Phoenix and he was acknowledged as a respectable community leader.

After World War II, things began to change in the world of chance, and former East Coast crime figures began taking a greater interest in West Coast gambling, legal and illegal. By 1955, Gus Greenbaum's wire operation in Phoenix was a thing of the past, and he had transferred his activities to Las Vegas, where he worked with Bugsy Siegel and other reputed crime syndicate figures.

After Siegel was slain in Beverly Hills, California, Gus Greenbaum managed the Flamingo Hotel and Casino on The Strip in Las Vegas until 1954. It was rumored that Greenbaum got in hot water with some crime syndicate members in early 1955 by refusing to manage the financially ailing Riviera, also on The Strip.

According to John Winters, Mrs. Greenbaum was frightened by her brother-in-law's activities and connections, and had warned him that she had received an anonymous telephone call in which the caller threatened to teach Gus a lesson. On April 27, while her husband, Charles, was at the racetrack, she bid a visiting daughter goodbye, and told her, "The next time you see me, I'll be dead." About 8 P.M. that evening, Mrs. Greenbaum was found dead by her husband as he returned from his day at the races. According to the medical examiner, she had been suffocated.

Six months after the murder of Mrs. Greenbaum, ex-Hollywood union extortionist and Al Capone hood Willie Bioff was blown up as he stepped on the starter of his pick-up truck. Bioff, who was known in Phoenix as William Nelson, had been living comfortably in the area under that fictitious name as part of the government's "alias program" for his testimony in convicting some of his old mob friends. Apparently these friends finally caught up with him.

According to Winters, the Maricopa County sheriff at the time, Cal Boies, said that several West Coast hoods, including a bomb expert, were spotted in town the weekend prior to the bombing, but there was insufficient evidence to connect them with the crime.

On December 11, 1957, the body of eighteen-year-old Nicky Johnson, scion of a wealthy Phoenix family, was uncovered by sheriff's deputies in the desert north of town. He had been shot in the head with a shotgun. He had been subpoenaed to testify about a shooting that involved the operators of the "Top of the World" prostitution establishment in Superior, Arizona. Maricopa County Sheriff Cal Boies reportedly told newsmen, "The word was out that Johnson was a squealer, a rat."

On December 2, 1958, a housekeeper entered the home of Gus Greenbaum, whose sister-in-law had been slain in 1955, and there discovered the bodies of Gus Greenbaum and his wife, Bess. Both had been knocked unconscious, then killed by having their throats cut.

Again it was rumored that Greenbaum, who had been persuaded to take the job at the Riviera, had fallen out of favor with the ownership and associates at the Riviera because of his drinking and skimming of profits.

It was a gory, professional job, and no one was charged with the murder.

Then, for a period of seventeen years it was quiet.

In February 1975, however, an accountant who was scheduled to testify the following day at a Maricopa County grand jury hearing into the activities of Ned Warren, land fraud specialist, was found with five bullets in him at an underground parking garage in Phoenix. The accountant's name was Edward Lazar, and he had been president of Consolidated Mortgage Corporation, a firm controlled by Ned Warren. After he had missed appointments in the morning and afternoon of February 19, his wife and business associates called the police, who eventually found his body in a dark stairwell of the parking garage on North Central Avenue. In what may be described as professional hit man thoroughness, four bullets had been pumped into his heart and a fifth fired into the back of his head. The investigation into Lazar's murder is still continuing.

Another crime syndicate execution occurred in October of 1975, when another FBI transplant "alias" was sent to his maker by the use of a plastic explosive. Known as Joseph Nardi, a joking, helpful neighbor at the Canlen House Apartments in Tempe, this ex-gambler and Chicago gangster was really fifty-two-year-old Louis Bombacino, whose testimony it was reported sent six Chicago mob figures to jail for gambling violations.

On October 6, at about eight-thirty in the morning, Bombacino started to back his newly leased Lincoln Continental out of the apartment parking lot when the molded plastic bomb, the type used to blow up bridges in wartime, exploded, shattering some seventy-five windows in the apartment complex, and left what was left of Bombacino draped over the twisted door in a junk pile that was once a fine automobile.

It was reported that the FBI helped Bombacino move to Arizona in 1967 after they had learned that a Chicago mobster had a contract out to kill him. Bombacino testified against his ex-pals in 1969, but he apparently wasn't located by those seeking revenge until October 1975. According to the Tempe police, the case is still open.

All of these murders were in some fashion or other associated with the Mafia or the syndicate.

All of these murders are unsolved.

Professional work is how law-enforcement officers view them.

Yet when reporter Don Bolles was bombed, the hit man was easy to find.

As was indicated by statements reacting to Don Bolles' murder, it was generally assumed that the bombing was connected to some form of organized crime. Among those suggested as possible perpetrators were such loosely defined groups as the Mafia, the Cosa Nostra, the syndicate, the organization, the Chicago mob, the New York mob, the Detroit mob, the Mexican connection, the Warren organization, the Jewish Mafia, the gambling interests, the racing interests, the Arizona "good ole boys," the real estate interests, the politicians, the Indian conspiracy, and others. Even President Gerald Ford assumed that Bolles was a victim of the so-called underworld.

Initially, the police were nearly certain that the basic motive for the bombing attack was an attempt to intimidate reporters and the news organizations who employed them. They suggested it was a warning to the Arizona news media to lay off organized criminal activity in the state.

The "revenge" motive was considered unlikely since Bolles had been away from investigative reporting for nearly a year. Police theorized it had to be something else. Either Don Bolles had stumbled on to some material which could prove devastating if it were published, or organized criminals were arrogantly demonstrating their power and contempt for law enforcement in the state.

The revenge killings of Bioff, Greenbaum, and Bombacino were carried out as disciplinary measures by the underworld on their own, and were not aimed at legitimate institutions or people.

It had to be something really big for organized crime to snuff the life of a newsman.

Yet, as the police delved deeper into the case, this theory began to lose favor. If the Mafia or the syndicate· or any big-time criminal element had put out a contract on Don Bolles would they have hired somebody like John Adamson to do the job? It didn't make sense, it didn't fit the pattern of a mob-style killing.

The contacts Adamson made with Bolles prior to the bombing, the number of people who were willing to talk about Adamson's activities, his local background and reputation, his involvement of others, and the

39

botched bombing job at midday in a well-observed parking lot seemed to suggest amateur night at the Borgias'. According to police theorists, the use of John Harvey Adamson as the contract killer caused them to abandon the Mafia intimidation of the news media concept as the primary motive, and search for a more logical reason.

After sifting through innumerable possibilities, those investigating the case came to the conclusion that the bombing was set up and carried out in the manner it was, either by crime syndicate members who wanted suspicion turned away from the mob and cast upon certain local people as part of a sophisticated power grab, or as the product of some Arizona criminal group whose acquaintanceship with professional killers was rather limited.

The logic of this conclusion was strengthened just two days after Don Bolles died when Phoenix attorney Neal Roberts, who had become embroiled in the case through his contacts and assistance to John Adamson, offered his theories on the bombing murder in exchange for immunity from prosecution.

Attorney Roberts suggested to police and prosecutors on June 15 that the Bolles bombing may have resulted from the frustration of millionaire Kemper Marley over his inability to get and hold an appointment to the state Racing Commission. He told the police that he had surmised this from conversations with Phoenix contractor Max Dunlap, a friend of Kemper Marley's.

Though the public wasn't informed of Roberts' theory until July 9, police knew on June 15, and it was filed as a supporting statement for Roberts' request for immunity with Superior Court Judge Roger Strand on July 7.

The evidence that the police were accumulating

seemed to fit Roberts' theory, and it eventually became the prosecution's contention in trying the case against those alleged to have perpetrated the murder of Don Bolles.

Chapter 3

THE ADAMSON TRIAL

At 1:30 P.M. on the day Bolles died, Phoenix police picked up John Harvey Adamson at his favorite watering hole, the Ivanhoe Cocktail Lounge. From the Ivanhoe, he was taken directly to the Phoenix police building on Washington Street, where he was booked for the bombing murder of the investigative reporter.

At 2:30 P.M., Adamson was transferred under heavy guard to the Maricopa County Jail.

At 4:15 P.M., he appeared before Superior Court Commissioner Chris Tauntas, who denied a release on bond for Adamson due to the nature of the charge.

Thus began the incarceration of John Harvey Adamson and the series of events which culminated in an agreement with the state of Arizona that was to save him from the gas chamber at the state prison. Known in jailhouse parlance as "copping a plea," the agreement would exchange a twenty-year sentence for an admission of guilt in the Bolles bombing and testimony indicting others in the murder and various other crimes.

John Harvey Adamson, age 33, is 6 feet 1 inch in height, and weighs in at approximately 214 pounds.

He was born in Chicago, moved to Phoenix as a child, and attended high school at Phoenix North, where he played trombone in the band and was president of the Latin Club.

In appearance, John Harvey Adamson is a flaccid, moon-faced hulk who fits Don Bolles' own description as a "sleazy bastard" to perfection. He wears his hair in a semi "Prince Valiant" bang down over his forehead, and continually sports a pair of sunglasses in the manner of a Beverly Hills hustler. Partial to garish sport shirts, his sartorial desires seem a cross between a "mod sale" at Penney's and a Duke Kahanamoku hand-me-down.

According to Paul Dean in the *Arizona Republic*, others have described him as "a big fat pussycat," "a houseboy for heavies," "a flake," "a backslapper," "a braggart," and "arrogant."

At a preliminary hearing, Texas lawyer Percy Foreman called Adamson "a coward who didn't have the courage to trigger the bomb himself," and Adamson himself concurred in this description. Adamson in testimony admitted planting the bomb under Bolles' car, but said James Robison actually triggered the device.

In 1962, he entered Arizona State University, where he was considered a mediocre student without much push. Reporter Charles Kelly of the *Republic* interviewed some of Adamson's fellow students and fraternity brothers (Phi Delta Theta) and came up with these comments:

"He was the kind of a guy who liked to take the wings off flies."

"He had a sadistic streak."

Kelly in his article tells of Adamson's fraternal nature. "During the fraternity's Hell Week—a hazing period for pledges—Adamson was a standout in the harassment department."

In Kelly's article, a college acquaintance remembers Adamson as the one who always stayed up all night with the pledges making them eat garbage and do push-ups. The fraternity brother recalled how Adamson seemed obsessed with a handgun, a .357 Magnum Smith & Wesson, that he kept in the frat house and was constantly cleaning. One time, this fraternity brother accompanied Adamson on a brief holiday to Pine, Arizona, where Adamson's parents had a cabin. He told how Adamson brought his handgun with him, and while they were walking near a dumping ground in the area spotted a skunk. John Harvey leveled his revolver and shot the animal. Though the first shot was sufficient, Adamson kept pumping bullets into the carcass. "He just kept shooting bullets into it, five or six times—that's kind of brutal!" the fraternity brother suggested.

In further reminiscences, it was recalled that Adamson was during his college days a member of the Maricopa County sheriff's posse, and made a big point of showing off his uniform, badge, and gun belt.

Later, when Adamson got a part-time job as an ambulance driver with the Green Acres Mortuary, he was fond of trying to impress his college chums by turning on the flashing lights and the siren whenever he had the chance to show off. He also enjoyed telling fraternity brothers gory stories about "scraping up bodies," and tried to entice one of them into the mortuary to "see some of the stiffs they were preparing for burial."

In 1966, Adamson married Saralou Combs, an ASU coed whom he dated while in high school. He dropped out of college in his senior year and took an insurance job with his father-in-law. The marriage, and the job, didn't work out. After a series of job failures, he was divorced from his first wife and later married his present wife Mary, a nurse.

In the years between the end of his first marriage and his arrest, not much is known on how he made his money. He did work as an ambulance driver and operated a service that towed away illegally parked cars,

45

but the main source of his revenue remains a mystery. Whatever he did for money was profitable, for he was able to skeet-shoot, spend money at the racetrack, involve himself with the breeding of racing dogs, and maintain his "lounge lizard" boozing habits at the substantial rate of a quart a day.

An article in the *Arizona Republic* said, "As events moved toward the Bolles killing, Adamson was trying to promote himself as a qualified hood. He bragged to his friends who hung out with him at the Ivanhoe Lounge and the Phone Booth bar in the Del Webb building that he sold stolen clothes as a front for his true trade: that of an arsonist."

With Adamson safely in jail, due to his incredibly stupid actions prior to the bombing and the fine investigative work by the Phoenix police which corroborated the evidence of these actions, the search turned to those who ordered and paid for his services.

Rumor mills were grinding their grist to capacity, and while the police went about the laborious job of sifting presentable facts, the news media, particularly the Pulliam press, was turning the reportorial spotlight on every alley of possibility.

Anyone who had any connection with John Harvey Adamson was interviewed and reinterviewed.

The business dealings of attorney Neal Roberts received considerable scrutiny, and his associations were well publicized.

In addition, the Bolles murder did produce an upsurge in both media and police investigation of crime in the state. Land fraud, political corruption possibilities, and organized crime all became the subjects of intensive inquiry. Both the national and Arizona news organizations were caught up in an anti-crime fervor that verged on a crusade.

Meanwhile, in his isolated jail cell, John Harvey Adamson basked in the worldwide publicity, smugly certain that those who employed him could pull the strings to get him off with a slap on the wrist. When questioned if the Mafia was behind him, Adamson reportedly told police officers, "The people behind me are worth a hell of a lot more than forty acres of garlic." So it was with an air of quiet confidence that he entered Justice of the Peace Marion Reno's well-guarded courtroom on June 21, 1976, for his preliminary hearing. "What could they prove?" he may have thought. "So I got Bolles to come to the Clarendon—so what?"

Little did he suspect that his girl friend and one of his good buddies were ready to testify, to save their own hides from possible prosecution.

After attorneys Mickey Clifton and Stephan Scott were not retained, and court-appointed attorney Stephen Gerst decided that discretion was the better part of valor, a firm of three young lawyers—Greg Martin, William Feldhacker, and William Friedl—was appointed by the court to handle Adamson's defense. They met him for the first time just a few hours before the preliminary hearing was to begin.

At the prosecution table sat William Schafer III from the state attorney general's office and Gene Neil, a deputy county attorney. Technically the case was to be handled by the Maricopa County attorney, as is the normal jurisdiction for murders that occur in the city of Phoenix. However, due to the nature of the case with its global publicity, the political and judicial powers that be had decided that Deputy Attorney General Schafer would be the chief prosecutor, temporarily assigned to the county attorney's office, and Neil, a regular deputy county attorney, would assist. To simplify, the state of Arizona had taken de facto charge of the case, with County Attorney Moise Berger's apparent cooperation. It was obviously felt that the county attorney's competence to handle such a trial was insufficient.

Fort Knox had nothing on the security established that morning at the Maricopa County Court building. Long before the hearing began the eighth floor had been "swept" by law enforcement technicians. Sheriff's deputies had searched every conceivable nook and cranny, under chairs and benches, in wastebaskets, any possible place that a weapon or a bomb might be secreted. A metal-detecting device used to spot hijackers had been borrowed from American Airlines and was set up at the entrance to the courtroom, and when some twenty-five to thirty authorized members of the news media arrived, they were thoroughly searched before they were allowed to enter.

At 10:12 A.M. Justice of the Peace Marion Reno sat down behind the judicial bench and the hearing began.

The opening gambit came from Adamson's defense table. A motion was filed to "clear the court of newsmen and spectators on the grounds that preliminary evidence might be presented that could present a clear and present danger to a fair and impartial trial for our client."

The motion was denied, and the first witness was called.

Homicide detective George Kletlinger took the oath and began reciting the story of occurrences at the bombing scene on the day of the blast. He told of the wrecked car and described other details of the scene, and related the testimony of witnesses. Over defense objections he was able to testify how several of those at the scene heard the injured Don Bolles mutter the name John Adamson while sprawled next to his car. Mostly Kletlinger's testimony regarded the physical evidence at the scene, and through it all Adamson sat seemingly unconcerned, his arms folded across his chest, peering through his dark glasses. Every now and

48

then he would whisper something to his defense counsel or look over at the press section, as if he were counting noses.

With the conclusion of detective Kletlinger's testimony, Judge Reno ordered a luncheon recess.

At 2 P.M., court reconvened.

The first witness in the afternoon session was an attractive thirty-year-old divorcee, Gail Owens. As she nervously took the witness box dressed in a simple vee-striped cotton frock with her long wavy auburn hair obviously groomed for the occasion, John Adamson looked surprised and a bit discomforted as he slumped in his chair.

It was the first noticeable emotional response from Adamson.

Under questioning from Deputy County Attorney Gene Neil, Mrs. Owens began to reveal her relationship with Adamson and the details of a trip she took with him to San Diego, California. She said they had met for the first time some seven months earlier, and had met periodically since then. On April 20, 1976, after spending the night at a Holiday Inn in Phoenix, they drove to San Diego in Mrs. Owens' Chevrolet Monte Carlo.

"In San Diego, we registered at the King's Inn in Mission Valley under the name of J. Owens," she recalled.

"The next day we drove to a hobby shop," she explained, "where Adamson told a sales clerk he wanted to buy a present for his brother." When they left, she said Adamson was carrying something in a box, "about the size of a shoe box."

Questioned as to whether she knew what was in the box, Mrs. Owens testified that several days later in their hotel room in San Diego she looked inside the package and saw a "radio control device—it was

49

a box which had knobs on it, with two little boxes, and there were wires."

By the time of Adamson's preliminary hearing, Phoenix police had determined that the bomb which killed Don Bolles was triggered by a radio-controlled device.

"After we got back from San Diego, he [Adamson] asked me if I knew Don Bolles," Mrs. Owens testified. "I said yes, I thought he was a reporter for the newspaper."

She continued, "The following day, he asked me if I'd go down to a bar on First Avenue and Van Buren, and see if I could see Bolles. So, the following day I went down—Brookshires, I think it was—went in, and had a drink," she said. "I didn't see Don Bolles—I believe I asked someone if reporters went into Brookshires, but no one knew."

Mrs. Owens under intense questioning revealed that Adamson bragged that he had a job in which he could earn "a lot of money."

"He made the remark, something to the effect that he had a job coming up where he was going to make a lot of money," she told the court, "and if that one went well, he'd have two more."

On the day of the bombing, in the early afternoon, "he called me," she testified, "and said, 'Something's happened and I won't see you for a while.'"

Gail Owens' testimony concluded late that afternoon, and the third witness in the preliminary hearing was called to the stand. He was Robert Lettiere, an erstwhile friend of John Harvey Adamson's.

Lettiere is an ex-convict who raises racing greyhounds in partnership with Adamson, and apparently was a confidant.

Upon swearing in, Lettiere immediately invoked the Fifth Amendment.

Lettiere's attorney, Louis A. Moore, Jr., stood up,

apologized to the court for being dressed in the uniform of a softball player—he didn't have time to change—then told the judge that Lettiere would continue to invoke his right not to provide testimony that might tend to incriminate him unless he was given immunity.

After a conference with the prosecution, Judge Reno told Lettiere that since the state had agreed to extend immunity in this case, he was going to order him to testify. The defense attorneys objected on the grounds that no formal papers granting immunity had been presented by the state, but Reno overruled their objections and explained to Lettiere that by ordering him to testify, he would receive immunity from prosecution for such testimony provided he did not lie.

After a brief consultation with his lawyer in the softball uniform, Lettiere nodded his agreement to the judge, and his testimony began.

The questioning brought out the startling allegation that Adamson had admitted bombing Bolles' car.

According to Lettiere, he and Adamson were sitting on a bench in front of Lettiere's home the night after the bombing and Adamson said, "That was a hell of a charge I built under that car, I can't understand how the man lived. If I ever get [blow up] another foreign car, I'm going to make damn sure it's not a Datsun," Lettiere quoted Adamson as saying.

Lettiere's testimony also told how Adamson had invited him to take a drive down to the parking lot of the *Republic* and *Gazette* building on the Friday before the bombing, and en route told him that his "people" or his "partners" had a job planned, and that he was going to blow up a car. Adamson said that he was going to get $10,000 for the job, and would get more for future jobs, according to Lettiere.

When they arrived at the parking lot across from the newspaper plant, Lettiere said, Adamson asked the security guard on duty where to find the car of a "Don something" and that he had some papers to put in the vehicle. According to Lettiere, the guard said it was all right to look around but they couldn't find the little white Datsun, so they left with Adamson remarking, "Well, I couldn't do anything here, anyway."

From the R&G parking lot, they drove to a Datsun dealership on East Camelback. On the way, Lettiere said, Adamson offered him 10 per cent of the money if he would "keep tabs on the guy in the white Datsun."

"I told him, 'No. It's not my bag. I'm not interested in it,'" Lettiere said.

At the Datsun dealership, Adamson looked over some Datsuns, checking under the hood and underneath the vehicles, he told the court.

Lettiere's damaging testimony concluded, some thirteen hours after the hearing began, after which Justice of the Peace Marion Reno said simply, "It is apparent to this court that probable cause has been established, and you will be held to answer in Superior Court."

When the testimony of the preliminary hearing was published, public reaction indicated a satisfaction that the Bolles hit man was indeed in custody, but—who was behind it? This question was paramount, and conspiracy theories were conceived to include almost every part of the Arizona establishment.

Politicians are usually considered fair game, and with election-year polls indicating that public trust of politicians had reached a new low, the Bolles bombing did nothing to enhance their images in the state.

The day after Don died, Congressman Sam Steiger requested an interview with the Phoenix police. He told news media representatives, "I telephoned them! The meeting was my idea, and I'm willing to answer any questions because I don't want them [meaning the police] chasing rabbits. I want them to get the man who blew him [Bolles] away."

Steiger said he had canceled two days of Washington appointments so that he could help the investigators, and wanted to reaffirm earlier statements that he had never had business or social dealings with Ned Warren, Sr., the subject of some of Don Bolles' investigative articles. "I met Warren once, many years ago when I was having lunch at Applegate's. I hadn't seen him before, haven't seen him since, and have had absolutely no dealings with the man."

Steiger acknowledged that his office had answered a letter requesting " a Forest Service land transfer" from a company operated by Warren. "That request," he said, "came on Consolidated Mortgage stationery, was signed by Emanuel Singer, and Ned Warren's name did not appear on the document. I didn't even know Consolidated was controlled by Warren until years later. It was a simple, routine request, one we answer for anyone."

The obviously hurt and irate congressman continued, "I'm angry, frustrated, and very upset at implications that I had anything to do with Don Bolles' death. God! Don was a close friend and we worked together on the same side in the fight against Emprise. If there hadn't been a Don Bolles there wouldn't have been any Steiger versus Emprise for the past six years."

In a voice filled with emotion, he continued, "Since the bombing, every time my name appears in the paper I lose a hundred volunteers for my campaign for the U. S. Senate, and I can't blame them. Hell, I wouldn't want to have anything to do with a politician who mixed with hoods."

Steiger also announced that he never was involved in "any kind of deal, land or any other business" with Barry Goldwater or Harry Rosenzweig.

This Steiger denial received support from Rosenzweig, who, according to the *Republic*, in a separate interview said, "I don't know why my name was mentioned. There has never been at any time any real estate deal which involved Barry Goldwater, Sam Steiger, and myself."

Rosenzweig added that he recently visited Goldwater, who was recuperating from hip surgery at Good Samaritan Hospital. "He's still wondering [about the business relationship] too."

Republican politicians were not the only ones to be viewed with suspicion. Mafia support was rumored for Democrat Dennis DeConcini (now U.S. senator), Governor Castro's financial backing by the wealthy Kemper Marley was viewed with concern, and even the most popular Democrat in the state, Attorney General Bruce Babbitt, was attacked.

As far as the reputation of the Arizona state Legislature was concerned, some individuals received lukewarm praise, but as a body it was considered weak, ineffectual, and not beyond subservience to unethical and criminal elements with sufficient money and clout.

The general distrust of politicians was amplified in Arizona by the Bolles murder for two reasons:

1. For a year prior to his death, Don Bolles had been working on politics and the Arizona Legislature. This suggested to some that the cause of his death must have had some political connection.

2. The mere fact that Bolles was interested enough to meet twice with Adamson, who alleged political corruption by Goldwater, Steiger, and Rosenzweig, gave some the idea that where there's smoke, there's fire, even though Bolles himself believed the information was phony and told others of this conviction.

In addition, the Phoenix area had acquired what may be termed an anti-establishment bias over the past few years due principally to Watergate, the defeat of the establishment-supported Charter Government Committee in Phoenix, and the problems that stemmed from an inability to bring land fraud specialist Ned

Warren to trial. Other factors which had caused a general malaise toward the status quo powers in the community were the milk and bread price-fixing scandals, the collapse of the Lincoln Thrift Association, and the obvious increase in drug traffic and abuse in the state.

The accumulated reaction to festering problems, topped off by the Bolles assassination, created a mild paranoia in which current leadership in most any field was suspect.

Since Phoenix is both the state capital and Arizona's major population center, the attitudes which gain ascendancy here generally dominate the total Arizona scene. As a result, most of the problems in the state were ascribed to weaknesses spawned by the controlling power of the Phoenix area's establishment.

The revelations of land fraud which preceded the Bolles murder, and other criminal scandals, suggested ineffective law enforcement and anemic prosecutorial efforts in relation to white collar crime, both by the state government and Maricopa County, which houses the Phoenix metropolitan complex. The Maricopa county attorney's office in particular started receiving heavy criticism from a variety of sources in early 1975.

The county attorney, Moise Berger, who was serving his second four-year term, had been battling with the board of supervisors during most of his tenure in office over funding and operation of his office, but criticism peaked in September after his office was unable to prosecute land frauder Ned Warren. Toward the end of the previous month, Berger had asked that charges against Warren be dropped because his chief witness against Warren had lied at the preliminary hearing.

On September 10, the powerful group of Phoenix businessmen known as the Phoenix Forty issued a statement which accused Berger of being ineffective and disruptive to the process of criminal justice. Though the statement didn't call for his immediate resignation, it said, "In our opinion, Mr. Berger neither capably administers his office nor merits the continued confidence of this community."

Berger counterattacked by implying that certain powerful elements in the community were hindering him in his attempts to prosecute white collar crime and fraud.

The pressures on the county attorney mounted, but he remained in office until after the Bolles murder and the prosecution of John Harvey Adamson began.

Normally, it would be the Maricopa county attorney's office which would handle the prosecution of a murder trial in the Phoenix area, but in short order, the state attorney general entered the arena, and after consultation with County Attorney Berger, William J. Shafer III, a member of Attorney General Bruce Babbitt's staff, was appointed to head the prosecution team in conjunction with members of Berger's county office. Though technically within the province of the Maricopa county attorney, the appointment of Schafer to head the prosecution team was a de facto takeover of the case. Shortly thereafter, Moise Berger resigned.

While Berger had been under fire for over a year, an incident occurred shortly after the Bolles assassination which not only created consternation in Arizona's legal community but in the state's general establishment. And it provided the reason or excuse, depending upon the point of view, to call for Berger's resignation.

This incident was the publication of a tape-recorded interview between Phoenix detective Lonzo McCracken and Berger.

In a *New York Times* article on June 14, 1976, statements from that recorded interview were presented though the names of the participants were not used. According to the *New York Times*, a senior prosecutorial official of the Maricopa county attorney's office (later revealed in publications as Moise Berger) said that he had not been able to prosecute more aggressively because of what he called a "power coalition" of interests that blocked such prosecution and kept his staff too small to be effective.

He said that a well-known businessman and Republican party leader headed the coalition and further stated, "You can't get work done. Cases get thrown out of court and you don't understand why. The lid is on . . . all the way from the very top," he said.

According to the *New York Times*, the senior official also conceded that he had had a sexual affair with a secretary employed by two of the land companies that he was investigating. It was reported that Phoenix police believed that the senior official was being blackmailed by these companies as a result of the affair, since the official was a married man.

Berger later denied he had made the statements attributed to him, but Phoenix police detective Lonzo McCracken in commenting for the record stated that Berger was the senior official on the tape and that he (McCracken) was the detective that did the interview.

"He's lying to the paper here," McCracken said. "He said it, there's no doubt about that."

Berger's resignation was warmly received by the establishment, and Phoenix Forty spokesman James Simmons said, "We have been concerned about the leadership in that office for some time . . . I think a change is welcome."

The resignation in July did not take effect until the middle of August, at which time Deputy County Attorney Donald W. Harris was appointed to fill out Berger's unexpired term, a matter of some four and a half months. It was widely assumed that Harris would merely "baby-sit" the office, handle routine prosecutions, and leave such important matters as the Adamson case to the attorney general.

Harris proved a surprise.

Donald W. Harris is an ex-Marine Corps officer with extrovert tendencies who apparently took his interim appointment as Maricopa county attorney as a mandate to fight crime in the Phoenix area regardless of whose ox was gored. Rather than doing the expected, Harris took charge of the county attorney's office like a military commander entrusted with a "do or die" commando mission. He opened the doors of his office to the public, and announced that the door would remain open to any and all who wished to speak with the county attorney. He told the news media that he would be open and candid to their questions, and though he only called one news conference during his tenure he was constantly the subject of interviews by individual members of the media. And he was far from timid in commenting on the Adamson case or the status of crime in the state.

Harris ignored the mounting pressure that was being exerted by prosecutors and the business community to cut down on the national publicity the state was receiving. Instead, he responded to news media inquiries with colorful, pithy, and sometimes rather startling comments. For example, on the CBS news program "60 Minutes," Harris hit hard at the old established members of Arizona's controlling elite. He stated that there was corruption in Phoenix and that organized crime had moved into the state. This he blamed on the "decay from within." "They always talk about our Italian enemies, the Mafia and everything—and I'm sure they're around," he said, "but they don't disturb me as much as the 'Joneses' and the 'Smiths,' the good old Anglo-Saxon names. I think those are some of the people we should start looking at—and worrying about."

When queried by CBS's Morley Safer, County Attorney Harris responded to a question on the possible motive for the Bolles bombing by saying that he thought Don Bolles was killed because he was on to some big local figure who was an old-timer and very wealthy, and this person just couldn't "stand the heat." He responded to a question on John Harvey Adamson by saying, "Of course, we feel he was involved in the homicide—he partook in it—and he set Don up."

Harris then went on to say that what he really wanted, however, was to get the persons who paid to have it done, and indicated to Safer that he had information relating to this, and also had received information from others who were willing to trade off lighter sentences for themselves in exchange for putting somebody in the death house.

He also went along with the prevailing theory that it was not the Mafia or any nationwide crime syndicate that had Bolles killed, but still believed it was done to intimidate the news media. He said that Bolles, he believed, was "done in" as an example, a gesture to the news media to stop looking into crime in the community, but was primarily done at the behest of Arizona-born criminal elements. He also pointed out the amateurism of the murder plot and said it was done by a "punk," and not by a true professional.

Harris' candor was not just confined to news media interviews; he didn't hesitate to mount the rostrum and state his views to members of the Arizona establishment itself.

In addressing the Scottsdale Bar Association at a meeting in the Safari Hotel, Don Harris told the lawyers of this wealthy Phoenix suburb on September 14 that the Phoenix area was a haven for gangsters and criminals who have ties with civic leaders and public officials, and offered the opinion that there was little hope the situation would be cleaned up in the near future. He said that organized crime interests have financial ties in Maricopa County that are so strong that eradication of crime was nearly impossible.

"I don't see things getting better," Harris was quoted by the *Arizona Republic* as saying. "I'm really disappointed and depressed about what I have found," he reportedly told the assembled lawyers.

Again he reiterated that organized crime interests could not have gained a foothold in Arizona without help from public officials, real estate boards, and other respected leaders and institutions. "Everybody is tied in with land deals," he asserted, explaining that land fraud had become rampant in the state because land transaction permits such lucrative rake-offs.

These comments to the Scottsdale Bar Association were mere soup and salad compared to his meatier statements to follow. Harris said he was considered a "safe guy," but since taking office acknowledged that he had made a lot of people uncomfortable. To point up this comment, he said that he had been asked by a judge, a civic leader, and an aide to a national political figure to take it easy on his criminal investigations. He refused to name them, however.

"Last week I got my first death threat," he told the audience, and said the sum total of the threat was that he should have been killed instead of Don Bolles.

To cap off the evening, he took on the powerful *Republic* and *Gazette* newspaper combine by asserting that President Richard Nixon in 1972 personally placed a telephone call to the *Arizona Republic* asking that a criminal investigation of a national leader by reporter Don Bolles be called off . . . and according to Harris, it was. Harris continued, saying that the files on this particular case had disappeared from the county attorney's office, which meant that there was now not enough evidence to prosecute the case. Harris mentioned in passing that this same politician was also being investigated by the Phoenix police.

(In an article on September 15 the *Arizona Republic* quoted its executives and editors as saying that Harris' statements were not true, and that no conversation took place between *Republic* executives and President Nixon about investigations being carried on by the newspaper.)

As a result of these and other statements by Maricopa County Attorney Donald W. Harris, ruffled feathers were the uniform of the day from Sun City to Apache Junction, especially in the paneled cubicles of the legal establishments and the carpeted offices of Phoenix's higher echelons of power.

Morley Safer on "60 Minutes" aptly described Phoenix as "the nation's biggest small town." And, as he suggests, despite its big-city pretensions the average Phoenician is more comfortable with a dung-encrusted cowboy boot than a ballet slipper. Phoenix's establishment, its powerful elite, is also small-town in that its social alliances of merchants, bankers, farmers, ranchers, and lawyers are able to maintain a favorable climate toward their respective enterprises through their contacts in state and local governments. The old-line families and enterprises still run the show despite the influx of outsiders.

While Maricopa County Attorney Harris aggravated a number of powerful people with his allegations, he was by no means alone in his condemnation of the lingering past.

On the same program, CBS's "60 Minutes," one member of an old-line Arizona family, Arizona Attorney General Bruce Babbitt, committed what may be considered heresy in some quarters in his response to a question if the so-called Arizona establishment had been able to keep a lid on investigations in the state.

Babbitt said, "Has the lid been on in Arizona? The answer is yes!" He explained, "What I mean is that there has been an atmosphere in the state for some time that anything done by people wearing coats and ties goes. Anything that purports to be business is not

61

to be critically examined. State government exists for the purpose of facilitating business deals, not regulating them, and the police and criminal justice system is there for the purpose of handling burglars and people who carry guns."

While the statements made by Donald Harris and Bruce Babbitt made great news copy, and many heads nodded in agreement, these general allegations were of little concern compared to a more specific problem, the investigation into the Bolles murder and the trial of John Harvey Adamson. Never had the state of Arizona been confronted with a case of this magnitude, and among those with influence in its justice system it was "nail-biting time."

After the quick apprehension of Adamson, it was felt that any major "goof" in the Bolles investigation or the trial of his murderer could result in a chaos that might provoke federal intervention on a massive scale. Some could visualize congressional committees arriving by the score, full-blown Justice Department investigations of state government, and a spotlight of attention that would rip asunder the fabric of the status quo and damage the state's vested interests beyond repair. Among politicians and the judiciary in Arizona, the temper of the times was an apprehension bordering on paranoia.

Adamson entered his plea of innocent on July 2, and a trial date was set for September 2. On August 12, Superior Court Judge David Perry granted a delay in the trial until October 1. Judge Perry was among the first of many judges who were assigned to juggle the "hot potato" for a while, then toss it to another. On October 18, 1976, the case was in the hands of Superior Court Judge Frederic Heineman, and jury selection began.

During the first half of October, tensions building in the state's justice community were kept from public view, but as the trial date approached criticisms of County Attorney Harris in particular were suggested to members of the news media by worried members of the legal profession. The volume and kind of publicity resulting from media interviews with the county attorney created a fear that Harris was cleverly manipulating the news media with or without intent to create either a lynching atmosphere which would assure a guilty verdict, or one that would nearly assure an acquittal on appeal. Possibly, some cynical critics suggested, all the talk was part of a plot to get Adamson out of the mess by abrogating his constitutional right to a fair and impartial trial. Others, particularly within the business community, were fearful that Harris' comments might simply expose to public view more of Arizona's dirty laundry.

The CBS program "60 Minutes," previously quoted, was aired and shortly thereafter Adamson's defense lawyers launched the campaign against the publicity. On October 20, Harris received a subpoena to testify at a closed hearing in the judge's chambers on a defense motion to call for a mistrial due to the publicity surrounding the case. He arrived at the hearing armed with a videotape of the CBS program on which he had appeared. According to Harris, Judge Frederic Heineman did not admonish him but simply said, "use your discretion," in reference to public statements. It was also reported that Harris revealed to the judge his plans to go ahead with a grand jury probe of the Bolles killing, and to seek other indictments.

It was clear from the time Harris took office in August that he was going to take a genuine interest in the Bolles killing and the Adamson trial, and despite the fact that the previous county attorney, Moise Berger, had agreed to let the attorney general's man, William Schafer, head up the prosecution against Adamson, it was also clear that Harris was not going to relinquish his overall control of the case.

Behind the scenes, Arizona Attorney General Bruce Babbitt, unhappy with Harris' increasing interest in the case, began to make contingency plans.

On the morning of October 21, the mess hit the fan.

Adamson's defense lawyers were in court formally introducing their motion for a mistrial when, according to the *Arizona Republic*, William Schafer, the member of the attorney general's staff who was acting as chief prosecutor in the Adamson case, was "pulled out of the courtroom by an angry Harris."

The report of this incident is somewhat controversial since Harris said it happened and Schafer said it didn't.

Harris said in an interview about the events of the day, "In the morning is when I had my 'shoot out' with Schafer. That's when I told him, you know, *you* are not running this case, and if need be, I'll make some changes."

Schafer contradicted the Harris version and the report by saying, "He never dragged me out of the courtroom—it never happened that I know of! He may have done it with Gene Neil [the assistant prosecutor], but it wasn't me." Schafer further elaborated, "As to the 'you're not running the case' conversation, there was no such conversation—there never was a shoot-out!"

Confrontation or not, on October 21 the relationship between Maricopa County Attorney Donald Harris and Arizona Attorney General Bruce Babbitt had reached the point of rupture.

That same morning, Attorney General Babbitt prepared a letter for the governor's signature which authorized him officially to take over the prosecution of the Adamson trial, took a plane for Tucson, and hand-carried it to Governor Raul Castro, who was attending a meeting in that city. Governor Castro was hesitant at first, and questioned whether he had the legal authority to do what Babbitt was asking. But with Babbitt stressing the urgency of the matter, the governor excused himself from the meeting, and accompanied by the young attorney general, headed for the nearby University of Arizona Law School library, where the governor could research the matter for himself.

Meanwhile, back in Phoenix, as the afternoon session of the Adamson trial began, the chief prosecutor, William Schafer, stood up and told the judge that the prosecution agreed with the defense contention that a mistrial should be declared because of the publicity. Schafer gave his reasons for this action later by saying, in obvious reference to County Attorney Harris, "A prosecutor is not permitted ethically to comment on evidence or his feelings about a case."

In Tucson, Governor Castro, a former judge and prosecutor himself, after consulting the Arizona statutes, still hesitated, but listened while Bruce Babbitt argued that it was necessary for him to take the case to prevent a mistake that might cause irreparable damage to it. Babbitt outlined for the governor the problems he contended that Schafer was having as he tried to maintain control of the prosecution. He reportedly told the governor, "Trust me, I know what I am doing." Castro mulled it over a bit longer, then signed the letter.

That afternoon Maricopa County Attorney Donald W. Harris was ousted from the case. The Phoenix police were contacted immediately and ordered to remove the files of the Adamson case from the county attorney's office. By five o'clock that afternoon, all the files and material pertaining to the case were gone. Outraged and angry, Harris at that moment could do little but pout.

In Superior Court, Judge Frederic Heineman declared that the Adamson case, which had merely reached a stage where the process of jury selection had begun, was a mistrial. Since there had been no testimony in the case, the only real effect this had was to cause a discharge of that particular panel of jurors and have another created. The charges were not being dropped, and another trial was scheduled.

Was this the end of Donald Harris' participation in the Bolles murder investigation? Not quite!

Infuriated by the events, the volatile interim county attorney called the action by the attorney general and the governor illegal, and prepared to take his ouster to the state Supreme Court. He also let the news media know, in no uncertain terms, exactly how he felt on the subject. Harris, in a lengthy interview in a college-oriented weekly newspaper, the *New Times* of Tempe, Arizona, revealed that he had asked the U. S. Justice Department to investigate his disputes with Attorney General Babbitt and Governor Castro. He charged that the attorney general's office had bungled the Adamson case and the entire Bolles murder investigation—"perhaps beyond repair." He said homicide detectives from the Phoenix Police Department told him that they were miffed by the way Assistant Attorney General William Schafer had ordered them off certain facets of the investigation.

Harris also alleged that Babbitt grabbed the case away from him in a quest for bigger and better things politically, and to carry out the wishes and desires of the *newspapers* in the community. He said that he didn't believe all those responsible for the Bolles murder would be caught or brought to justice, because of the way the attorney general was handling the matter. He revealed that he had talked to some informants who wanted to trade information on the murder for immunity, and that it was his understanding that Schafer had turned them down. He said that he was told by a private attorney who represented the informants that he (Harris) was removed from the case because he wanted to make a deal.

His legal attempts to get the Arizona state Supreme Court to overturn the action withdrawing the case from the county attorney's office failed, and his appeals for federal action apparently bore meager fruit. But his attacks and allegations caused many to wonder if political considerations had replaced a search for justice in the Bolles investigation.

With the prosecution of John Harvey Adamson safely within the province of the state attorney general's office, clear sailing to a proper and acceptable verdict was anticipated by a large segment of the state's legal fraternity. Publicity on the case was extensive, however, despite a sudden deacceleration of news coverage on the Bolles investigation by the *Arizona Republic* and the *Phoenix Gazette*. Suddenly on November 8, 1976, the prosecution changed its long-held opposition to a change of venue, and agreed with the defense that Adamson could not get a fair trial in Phoenix due to the massive amount of pre-trial publicity. Apparently it was felt that the ouster of Harris and a rising public resentment over delays in bringing the matter to trial had created an atmosphere in Arizona's largest city which would make it difficult to find jurors who could reach an unbiased verdict.

Five months had passed since Adamson's arrest, and an honest-to-goodness trial was still nowhere in sight.

Though both the defense and the prosecution now believed the change in venue was necessary, Judge Frederic Heineman disagreed and turned down the combined request on November 16.

While the "cat fight" over who would handle the prosecution was more or less settled, the problem of finding a competent, legally acceptable judge in Maricopa County re-emerged. On November 17, the defense attorneys for Adamson asked for a change of judge because, they alleged, Judge Frederic Heineman may have met Adamson socially some three years prior at a Phoenix restaurant they both frequented at the time.

Another factor, not mentioned in court by the defense attorneys but lurking in the background, was the fact that Judge Heineman had been picked up by the Phoenix police the previous weekend for drunk driving. Since Arizona's U. S. Senator Paul Fannin had been arrested by the Phoenix police on the same charge several years prior, the state had been somewhat hypersensitive to its public figures being picked up on this kind of charge. To many it seemed to indicate a lack of self-control and judgment necessary to a competent public official. Judge Heineman, testifying in his own defense at a hearing to determine his ability to continue with the case, told the court that he was *almost* certain that he had never met Adamson at the restaurant as alleged, but state Appeals Court Judge Donald Froeb after hearing the testimony granted the defense motion for another judge.

Almost immediately, Superior Court Judge Rufus Coulter was named to handle the Adamson case. A few days later, on November 23 Judge Coulter disqualified himself. Coulter explained that he had once represented L'Continental Restaurant while in private practice, a place at which John Adamson had once managed a car-towing operation. At the time, Adamson would haul illegally parked vehicles or cars which had overstayed their allotted time at the restaurant parking lot to a holding yard. He would then charge what some contend were exorbitant fees for towing them away. Coulter also indicated that he may have had some part in Adamson's divorce, and felt as a result that it wouldn't be ethical to hear the case, under the Canons of Judicial Ethics.

Superior Court Judge Warren McCarthy was then

assigned the Adamson trial, with the starting trial date set for November 29. McCarthy was assigned the case on November 23, and while the judge-swapping game was going on in Superior Court, the defense attorneys for Adamson had gone to the State Supreme Court with a special action which would halt further proceedings in Superior Court until the high court had reviewed the motions for venue change which Judge Heineman had turned down.

The reason for this special action was that under Arizona law the prosecution had to bring a defendant to trial within a period of ninety days. Delays caused by defense motions were not construed as part of this ninety-day period, but all of the prosecution hassles had prevented a start of the trial.

On November 24, Supreme Court Justice Jack D. H. Hays granted a stay in Superior Court proceedings in the Adamson case until the Supreme Court could review the change of venue decision issued by Judge Heineman against the wishes of both the defense and prosecution. This stay in effect stopped the clock just nine days before Adamson would have been "off the hook," according to Arizona law.

On December 7, a date some in Arizona believe will live in legal infamy, the Supreme Court of Arizona overturned Judge Heineman's decision and granted the defense and the prosecution a change in venue.

While both legal sides in the case favored the change, others in Arizona said the change was just political gimmickry to take the "heat" off the state, and make it more difficult for the national news media to cover the Adamson trial. It was pointed out that the well-publicized trials of Charles Manson, Sirhan Sirhan, and Patricia Hearst were held in the same locales the alleged crimes occurred, so why was it necessary to move the Adamson case to a smaller Arizona city or town? Smaller courtrooms in smaller cities with less facilities could have but one major effect, and this effect would be to prevent effective news coverage of the trial, it was suggested.

On December 9, Pima County (Tucson area) was selected as the new trial site, and Judge Ben C. Birdsall was assigned to the case. On Christmas Eve, Adamson was transported under heavy guard to Tucson. On December 28, jury selection began. On January 13, 1977, thirty-three jurors had been qualified to hear the case. On January 14, 1977, the trial of John Harvey Adamson was over—before it began.

Chapter 4

ADAMSON TALKS

As Judge Ben Birdsall peered down from his judicial bench in Tucson, John Harvey Adamson calmly confessed that he did indeed plant the bomb that killed investigative reporter Don Bolles. In an accompanying affidavit submitted that January 14, he also alleged that the bomb was actually triggered by James Albert Robison, a Chandler plumber, and that the "kill for pay" bombing was the result of a contractual agreement with Max Anderson Dunlap, a Phoenix building contractor, allegedly at the request of multi-millionaire Kemper Marley, Sr.

The confession by Adamson, it was revealed, was part of a deal, a plea bargain arrangement, whereby Adamson would escape the gas chamber for his confession and testimony implicating the others involved. Apparently, behind the scenes negotiations had been going on for a considerable period of time but only reached fruition on January 4, 1977, when Phoenix detective Jon Sellers was able to get the signed statement from John Harvey Adamson admitting his part in the bombing murder of Don Bolles. Ten days later, after all the details had been ironed out, it was presented as a fait accompli to Judge Birdsall in Tucson.

On that day, Phoenix police arrested both James Albert Robison and Max Anderson Dunlap as co-conspirators in the murder of Don Bolles—but, despite the statement from Adamson, the alleged perpetrator of the plot, millionaire Kemper Marley, Sr., was allowed to remain free, due apparently to insufficient evidence.

In the police affidavit filed with the murder complaint, Phoenix police detective Jon Sellers stated, "As a result of both my overall knowledge of the investigation and that specific information learned during the course of voluntary statements made in my presence by John Harvey Adamson which commenced on January 4, 1977, I do hereby state that there is reasonable cause to believe that Max Anderson Dunlap and James Albert Robison murdered Donald Bolles with premeditation and deliberation, and that Dunlap and Robison, as well as John Harvey Adamson, who is named in the complaint but not charged therein, conspired to commit the act of murder in the first degree."

It was also alleged in the affidavit that Adamson was asked by Dunlap to kill, in addition to Don Bolles, Arizona Attorney General Bruce Babbitt and King Alphonso (Alex Lizanetz) at the request of Kemper Marley. It also stated that Adamson and Robison had agreed to kill a fourth man, Doug Damon, at the instructions of Max Dunlap.

It was a bombshell in Arizona.

Though there was a general suspicion that a break in the case would occur, when it came it was a shock.

Suddenly the actions of the attorney general were construed as brilliant despite the legal circus that preceded the Adamson confession.

It soon became clear, however, that the real reason Adamson was willing to confess and turn state's evidence was the meticulously thorough and brilliant investigation conducted by the Phoenix Police Department.

In commenting on the police work, Captain Don Lozier of the Phoenix Police Criminal Investigation

Bureau spoke modestly but with a touch of pride. "I'd say we got *some* breaks in the case, but a lot of it was good information sources the investigating officers had, and a great deal of it was just some damned good investigative work. Timing became very important in this investigation. We employed a lot of strategy as to when we did a lot of things."

As an example of this strategy, Lozier remarked, "A lot of people couldn't understand why we didn't arrest John Adamson immediately after the bombing, but what these people didn't understand was that the most we could have charged him with before Bolles died was using an explosive device or assault with intent to murder—and he could have pled guilty to that. Then where would we have been?"

The Phoenix police captain recalled how early in the investigation there were many people who thought the investigation should have been handled by the federal government or some other agency, but "we held our ground and said no," he remarked, "and I think the Phoenix Police Department really came of age during that thing, and we really proved to people that we were capable."

"I'd put this investigation up against any investigation that was ever conducted in the United States," Captain Lozier emphasized. "It's made me extremely proud just to be associated with the Phoenix Police Department."

Yet, Kemper Marley remained free, and others simply could not believe what Adamson said was the gospel truth.

Piecing together John Harvey Adamson's version of the events presents a grotesque tale of evil incarnate. It tells of men so obsessed by a craving for power and money that the foulest deeds are within their ken. It tells of men devoid of conscience, amoral creatures who kill without emotion to satisfy their greed. It also tells of men who turn their backs on the victims of evil, pretend it doesn't exist, and consider themselves good citizens.

From evidence and testimony presented in court, it appears that John Harvey Adamson had acquired prior to the Bolles bombing a reputation as a punk who would do almost anything for money. (The state has agreed not to prosecute him for a number of crimes which include assault, arson, and another bombing attempt. A total of eleven specific crimes and all crimes that have been the subject of police reports were cited as "non-prosecutable" against Adamson in the deal.)

Events leading to the death of Don Bolles began during 1975 or early 1976, according to police.

Apparently Adamson and his associate, Jimmy "The Plumber" Robison, had been contacted by Phoenix contractor Max Dunlap and had agreed to kill a con man by the name of Doug Damon. Damon, it seems, had swindled Dunlap out of some $16,000 in a phony business proposition involving stolen silver bullion. The irate Dunlap wanted revenge, and Adamson and Robison agreed to make the hit. The interesting aspect of this meeting is that Adamson apparently introduced Dunlap to the con man, and initially involved him in the phony bullion swindle.

Phoenix attorney Neal Roberts, a former assistant attorney general, reportedly told police that he had introduced Dunlap to Adamson because he was "nefarious" enough to be interested in buying some stolen silver. According to Roberts, in this reported conversation, Dunlap told him that he would buy the stolen silver from Adamson's acquaintance. "Max came in and told me they had a deal whereby they were going to land at some airplane strip someplace and pick up this silver," Roberts reportedly told police in a sworn affidavit. "And it's my understanding that Max gave a friend of Adamson's some fifteen thousand bucks as a kind of earnest money and the guy never arrived with the silver. Now supposedly this whole transaction was being financed by Kemper Marley," Roberts is reported to have said.

Why Dunlap asked Adamson and Robison to kill Doug Damon, if Adamson had introduced him to the con man, has never been explained. Either Roberts or Adamson was lying to the police, or the full story wasn't revealed, or something, because knowledgeable law enforcement officers say, "It just doesn't make sense."

Many contend that there is little in the Bolles case or its periphery that makes sense. Perhaps Arizona is indeed a reincarnation of Alice's Wonderland, for there is nothing attributed to the Mad Hatter which cannot be surpassed by the reasons and motives for crimes which have surfaced as part of the overall investigation. Logic simply doesn't apply!

Important to the Adamson version, however, is the fact that he was introduced to Max Anderson Dunlap by attorney Neal Roberts, a friend. According to the police affidavit, Adamson said that he met Max Dunlap in March 1976 in front of lawyer Neal Roberts' office in Phoenix. During this meeting Adamson alleged that Dunlap asked him to kill Bruce Babbitt, the Arizona attorney general, and King Alphonso (Alex Lizanetz), a former Kemper Marley employee.

According to Adamson, Dunlap told him that the attorney general was investigating the liquor industry, and if he could not be persuaded politically to halt it, then Kemper Marley wanted Babbitt killed.

Alex Lizanetz, who calls himself "King Alphonso, a Robin Hood of All," was once employed by United Liquors as an advertising display man. United Liquors is owned by Kemper Marley. Since 1969 he has been writing letters to the news media and to various politicians condemning Kemper Marley and the owners of

Seagram's distilleries. Lizanetz accused Marley of a variety of criminal practices and spoke against him at a legislative hearing on Marley's appointment to the Arizona state Racing Commission.

According to Adamson, Marley wanted him killed because "he had given him a bad time in the past."

Two or three weeks after the request to kill Babbitt and King Alphonso, Adamson said he met Dunlap at the Ivanhoe Lounge, where Dunlap allegedly asked him to kill a third man, investigative reporter Don Bolles. According to Adamson, Dunlap said Marley wanted Don Bolles killed because he had given Marley a bad time, particularly over his appointment to the Racing Commission—and that Marley wanted Bolles to be killed first.

Adamson said that he nogotiated a package price for killing the three, Bolles, Babbitt, and Lizanetz, and the price was set at $50,000.

An extended look at the principals involved in the Bolles murder investigation reveals a cast of unlikely characters.

Neal Roberts: Neal Roberts is a forty-six-year-old attorney who was born in Houston, Texas, and grew up in Arizona. He graduated from North High in Phoenix the same year that Max Anderson Dunlap was class president.

Roberts then attended Phoenix College, the University of Arkansas at Fayetteville, and law school at the University of Arizona in Tucson, from which he graduated in 1955.

Admitted to the state bar of Arizona in 1955, he first entered private practice, then in 1959 joined the staff of Arizona Attorney General Wade Church as an assistant attorney general. That same year he was elected president of the Phoenix 20-30 Club, a community service organization. In 1960, he left the attorney general's office and re-entered private practice.

He first married prior to attending law school. This marriage broke up in 1962 with a separation, and his wife was granted a final divorce decree in 1967.

His second marriage occurred in 1969 when he wed a German-born model, Antje Bianca Samter. This marriage too headed for the shoals of matrimonial bliss and cracked up in 1976, when Antje filed for divorce.

Roberts is father and stepfather to a total of six children from the two marriages.

A friend and former client, Harry Noye of Lake Havasu City, says that Roberts has deteriorated in recent years and has begun drinking too heavily.

Though his estranged wife does not believe him capable of taking part in a murder plot, she is unable to explain his relationship with John Harvey Adamson. Asked why she thought Roberts associated with Adamson, Antje reportedly said, "I'll never know why he gets involved. Somehow, he seems to attract people who are scum, leeches. Yet, he's too bright for that kind of company."

Described as a man with an enormous ego, Roberts seems to exude a self-assurance bordering on self-adoration. One gets a feeling that he is contemptuous of those around him, and thoroughly convinced of his judgmental infallibility.

"His ego is what gets him into trouble," said a member of the news media who is well acquainted with Roberts' personality. "He thinks he can handle any situation, so he opens his mouth and talks too much."

Roberts was involved in a $5 million Canadian stock sale scandal in 1971, and is accused of participating in the bombing attempt of the building leased by the Bureau of Indian Affairs in Phoenix, a building in which he is a part owner.

Max Anderson Dunlap: Max Anderson Dunlap is a forty-seven-year-old building contractor and land developer who was born and raised in Arizona. He attended Madison Elementary School and North High, where he excelled in athletics and was known as a popular student.

Dr. Kenneth Olson, a psychologist-author and former Lutheran minister, was a boyhood friend of Max Dunlap's. He gives an intimate description of the youthful Max. "I remember Max had this infectious smile and laughter. He was so popular because he was just himself, no games and no phony. He ran for freshman class president in high school and just walked away with it, he was so popular," Olson recalled.

Referring to Dunlap's ahtletic prowess, Dr. Olson remembers, "Max hurt his knee in football, so he couldn't play football, but he lettered in varsity basketball and track as a freshman, which was very unusual in those days."

Olson told how he and Max Dunlap became good friends, a friendship that extended from elementary school through high school and after.

"We would spend Sunday afternoons in each other's homes just talking," he recalled, "and Max's big dream was someday to have his own land on which he could grow some crops and own some cattle."

Olson remembered that Dunlap came from a fine religiously oriented family, and disputed a published report in the *Arizona Republic* that Kemper Marley had raised him. According to the newspaper, Dunlap said that Kemper Marley, Sr., had raised him "almost like a son" after Dunlap's father died when Dunlap was twelve. Dr. Olson said this was ridiculous because he used to visit the Dunlap home almost every Sunday throughout Max's high school years, and he knew Max's father, who was in the insurance business. John

Savoy, a defense attorney for Max Dunlap, says that Max's father died when he was in his late teens.

After high school, Dunlap didn't go on to college but bought himself a small tractor and earned money by leveling lots and landscaping homes. When he had accumulated some money, Dunlap tried farming west of Phoenix and later near Yuma. "He was always undercapitalized," Dr. Olson recollects, "but it was his dream."

Dunlap married and became the father of seven children, five girls and twin boys. He has been married to the same woman for twenty-five years, and has the reputation of being a good father and a helpful neighbor.

Acquaintances describe him as a country boy type, who usually drives a pick-up truck.

Columnist Paul Dean accurately labeled him "more American Legion than country club."

While published reports have said that Dunlap's country boy façade is a cover for the true Dunlap, who is capable of illegal deals and doing just about anything, Dr. Olson says, "If I look back on the years I've known Max Dunlap, and as a psychologist who has worked with very many of the criminal element, Max would be the least potentially violent person I could possibly imagine."

Kemper Marley, Sr.: Kemper Marley, Sr., is a seventy-year-old Arizona millionaire. Born in Yuma, Colorado (not Arizona), he was the son of a successful rancher who moved to the Phoenix area.

Long influential in Democratic party politics, he is considered one of the "old-line" powers in Arizona. Active in business since 1927, he operated his father's interests until the elder Marley died in 1932, then expanded the business through diversified interests.

Harry Rosenzweig, a well-known Arizona businessman and political figure who says he has known Kemper Marley for sixty years, offered this comment, "I think he is the wealthiest man in the state. He made it! His father gave him a start, then he took something small and made it big," Rosenzweig said.

Among Marley's many interests is an ownership in land, farms, ranches, and other businesses in Arizona and Mexico.

He is president of United Liquors, a wholesale liquor business with annual sales in 1975 estimated at $15 million.

Rosenzweig estimates Marley's net worth at about $50 million, but other estimates range from $15 million to $1 billion.

Some rumors have circulated that he is in financial straits, but his vast holdings seem to belie this contention.

A mysterious figure, Marley lives unpretentiously in a modest home in Phoenix, and is described as a rugged Western-type individualist who likes to operate behind the scenes.

Often the silent partner in business deals, he makes money from money in a great variety of ways.

One police authority said, "There are rumors he has even loaned money in the past to Howard Hughes."

An entrepreneur with excellent Mexican connections, he is reported to be the principal stockholder in Maquinaria General del Occidente, a Caterpillar tractor dealership with headquarters in Ciudad Obregón, and reportedly owns land near Culiacán, the poppy-growing capital of Mexico.

Though implicated by the testimony of John Harvey Adamson and the theory suggested to police by Phoenix attorney Neal Roberts, nothing of indictable substance has apparently been turned up, since he has yet to spend a day in jail.

Roberts in his reported statement to the police said, "What I understand from Max, Kemper Marley is a man with a great deal of pride." He further suggested that Marley may have wanted some old-style Western justice for the Bolles article in the *Arizona Republic* which allegedly contributed to Marley's ouster from the Arizona State Racing Commission.

Number one on the tap list for campaign funds by Arizona politicians over the years, he is considered a man with enormous political clout. He was also the largest single contributor to Governor Raul Castro's 1974 gubernatorial campaign, and has helped fund numerous other state and county office campaigns.

James Albert Robison: James Albert Robison is a fifty-four-year-old, tough-looking, heavy-set man with a scraggly beard and a large scimitar-shaped scar on his forehead. He received the scar, it is said, from an awkward jackknife while diving into a swimming pool, hitting his head on the springboard while on the way down.

It is known he served in the Navy as a radioman until about 1946.

In 1948, he was initiated into the Plumbers, Steamfitters, and Refrigeration Local 280 in Pasadena, California. Since that time he has been fixing toilets and handling other equally dirty jobs.

Despite his rugged appearance, and his unglamorous though sometimes well-paid profession, Robison is more of a paradox than a stereotype. People from Robison's past have described him diversely as a violent tough guy involved in union quarrels and beatings, "not the straightest guy in the world, but a hell of a nice guy," and "a calming influence who enjoyed metal sculpture, reading, and current events."

He's an avid reader, and once, commenting on some court action during his preliminary hearing, said to one of the attorneys, "This reminds me of Ecclesiastes 3:16." In the paraphrased Living Bible, Ecclesiastes

3:16 says, "Moreover, I notice that throughout the earth justice is giving way to crime and even the police courts are corrupt."

Until he was jailed, Robison lived in a trailer in Chandler, Arizona, with his wife.

Neal Roberts, Max Dunlap, Kemper Marley, Sr., and James Robison—these are the four names most prominently mentioned in connection with the Bolles murder case, either as defendants or associated with defendants in the matter.

When John Harvey Adamson was called to testify in the preliminary hearing for Dunlap and Robison, he detailed his version of the events that led to the actual bombing.

After admitting that he planted the bomb, Adamson was asked by prosecutor William Schafer where the money to pay for the "hit" was going to come from. Adamson replied, "Max indicated that he had the key to the vault with Marley and that the money would be absolutely no problem."

According to a police affidavit, Max Dunlap met Adamson at Chauncey's Restaurant in Phoenix sometime during March and gave him $1,000 for expenses. Adamson said he again met Dunlap in April of 1976 and was given an additional $2,000 expense money.

On or about April 20, John Adamson testified, he went to San Diego, California, with his girl friend, Gail Owens. There he admittedly purchased the radio control device which was used to detonate the bomb under Bolles' car.

Returning to Phoenix, Adamson said, he and Jimmy Robison tested the radio control device and other components of the bomb. During May, testing and fabrication of the radio-activated bomb continued, according to Adamson's testimony, and he said he was in frequent contact with Max Dunlap, who urged him to kill Bolles as soon as possible.

"We've got to get this done," Adamson quoted Dunlap as saying. "Bolles is going to start on something in two weeks."

One week before the bombing, Adamson recalled on the stand that he called Don Bolles on the telephone and set up a meeting in the bar of the Islands Restaurant in Phoenix. He couldn't recall the exact day, but said that when he met Bolles late in the afternoon, the reporter mentioned that he had to attend the eighth-grade graduation of one of his daughters. During this fifteen-minute meeting, Adamson testified, he told Bolles a phony story about an informant supposedly living in San Diego who had proof that Congressman Sam Steiger of Arizona was involved with Emprise (a corporation often attacked by Steiger) and land fraud, and the possibility of the governor being involved was also great.

Adamson said Bolles didn't have time to continue the conversation, so they agreed to meet again if Adamson could get more concrete information from the fictitious informant.

The day before the bombing, Adamson said he called Bolles again and arranged a meeting for the next day, June 2, at the Clarendon House hotel. He told Bolles that the San Diego informant would be there at 11:15 A.M.

On the same day, Adamson said, he also called James Robison, who allegedly told him the radio-operated bomb was ready. Later that afternoon Robison delivered the bomb into Adamson's keeping at the parking lot next to the Ivanhoe Lounge, he told the court.

On the morning of the bombing, June 2, Adamson said that he and a friend, a one-legged ex-con named Hank Landry, went down to the Ivanhoe Lounge quite early, then drove to the office of attorney Neal Roberts. They arrived, he recalled, about 9 A.M. Unexpectedly, he said, he met Max Dunlap, whom he engaged in conversation on the lawn in front of Neal Roberts' office-home.

"I told him to tell Mr. Smith [a pseudonym for Kemper Marley] to go to the bank, that Don Bolles would be at the Clarendon House at eleven-thirty that morning and it would be over then," Adamson said.

"Good!" Dunlap replied, according to Adamson.

"I then left Roberts' office and went back to the Ivanhoe and drank cranberry juice until about ten fifty-five," he said.

In response to questioning Adamson continued his narrative. "I then went to a building at Third Avenue and Indian School Road [not far from the Clarendon House] and changed into some coveralls, a hat, and some gloves. Then I drove to the Clarendon House parking lot and met Jimmy Robison," he said.

According to the testimony, Adamson said they waited at the extreme south end of the parking lot.

"I wonder if he [Bolles] will be here?" Robison asked, according to Adamson.

After reassuring Robison that he would, they discussed their alibis.

"I'll be at the Ivanhoe," Adamson said he told Robison, and according to Adamson's testimony Robison indicated that he had worked up a story that he was out buying a plumbing part.

"About this time Bolles drove up and got out of his car," he said.

Bolles tried to get into the hotel through a parking lot gate, but couldn't, so he walked around the hotel building to the front entrance, Adamson continued. He then explained that he drove his car over to where Bolles had parked his vehicle, armed the bomb, got out and placed it under the driver's side of the little white Datsun, re-entered his car, and drove out of the parking lot. As he drove south on Fourth Avenue, he testified, he could see James Robison getting out of his pick-up truck some distance from the parking lot with the radio-operated detonating device and a pair of binoculars.

He told the court that he then drove to another parking lot, where he took off his coveralls, hat, and gloves. From there he drove to the parking lot next to the Ivanhoe, where he discarded the coveralls, hat, and gloves in a garbage container. He then entered the Ivanhoe, Adamson testified, where he placed a telephone call to Clarendon House and asked for Don Bolles.

When Bolles came on the line, Adamson said, "I told him that the individual from San Diego was hesitant and didn't want to be exposed. I also told him that I didn't have any more time to spend on it and I was sure he didn't either."

After hanging up the phone, Adamson said he waited until 11:30 A.M., then called a bartender at the Phone Booth bar in the Del Webb building not far from the Clarendon and asked if anything unusual had happened, and got no for an answer.

At about 11:35 to 11:40 A.M., Adamson said, he got a telephone call at the Ivanhoe from James Robison, who said, according to Adamson, "Tell Mr. Smith to go to the bank!"

"Is it done?" Adamson said he asked Robison.

"From eyeball to eyeball!" was the alleged reply.

Chapter 5

THE ATTORNEYS

"In another year, the Bolles death will be nothing more than a memorial basketball game," a former prosecuting attorney commented recently.

He was pointing out that the emotional impetus to rid the state of Arizona of its unethical and criminal elements will wane, and unless some newsworthy event such as the Bolles murder stirs up public anger, the business, political, and judicial climate of the state will revert to business as usual. Using the news media of the state as a barometer, the stories being served up to the public seem to verify this contention. As it was with Watergate and Nixon, Arizonans appear to be losing their zeal to clean up the state's organized and white collar crime. This is partly due to a natural ennui; a sustained emotional climate is difficult to maintain. But there is also evidence that much is being done by certain groups with the Arizona establishment to accelerate the reversion to so-called normalcy.

An editorial in the *Phoenix Gazette* entitled "Take a Look on the Bright Side" quotes the new head of the Arizona Bar Association as suggesting that Arizonans may be so concerned about problems and criticisms of the state that they are forgetting about its bright side. The editorial quotes Phoenix attorney Tom Tang as

saying, "Arizonans might easily fall victim to a nega-
tivism that could dim the state's future."

To those weary of news media bombardment on the
problems of crime in Arizona, editorials and statements
contributing to a relaxation of the apprehensive
feelings generated by the Bolles assassination are no
doubt welcome.

However, there are some who contend there is much
to be done before the state can let down its guard, particularly in cleaning up the practices of Arizona's lawyers.

Newly elected Maricopa County Attorney Charles
Hyder says, "The attitude of the state Bar Association
is—they really don't want to clean house! I've put in
many complaints on lawyers," Hyder said, "and constantly been told that an investigation was conducted
and they found no wrongdoing, even though they
hadn't contacted me [as to the charges]."

County Attorney Hyder believes there are discrimi-
natory practices against prosecutors by the controlling
hierarchy of the Bar Association.

"When the slightest complaint is made against a
prosecutor, however, you can rest assured that there
will be a full-scale investigation," he said. "Many lawyers are sour," Hyder emphasized, "and I'm one of
them!"

It is often suggested by law enforcement officials in
the state that behind every land fraud and white collar
scheme there is a member of the business community,
an unethical accountant, and an amoral if not unethical
lawyer. In addition, they suggest, the ability of wealthy
crooks to purchase the best legal talent available makes
it difficult to prosecute the worst offenders in white collar or organized crime.

Maricopa County Attorney Hyder, in referring to
the hassles and jurisdictional disputes in the handling
of the John Adamson case, said, "I think this case

above all cases will show you a breakdown in the criminal justice system." Hyder explained, "There may have been some philosophical differences about the way the case should have been handled, but nevertheless, the attorney general did not have the authority, as far as I am concerned, to step in on the case. Neither did the governor have the authority to take the case away from the county attorney's office," he added. "The statute is very clear," he said. "The only time that can happen is when the governor thinks there is a breakdown in the justice system—and I don't think that can be shown by the wildest stretch of the imagination in this case."

County Attorney Hyder backed up former County Attorney Harris and criticized the state's highest judicial body by saying, "Mr. Harris was right in challenging the governor's authority, and in my opinion—and I may get in trouble with the Bar Association for this— the Supreme Court was wrong in not accepting jurisdiction and clarifying the situation. They should have said, 'No! Mr. Governor, you cannot come in and take the case away, there hasn't been the showing required by the statute,' " Hyder emphasized.

"What's needed to make our justice system strong," he stressed, "is not to look at a case in its political context, which I feel they did. This was a big political hot potato—and we don't want to touch it," was the Supreme Court's reaction, according to Hyder. "They should have touched it!" he emphasized. Hyder continued, "If the Supreme Court of the United States would have adopted that attitude, Richard Nixon would still have been President of the United States."

What appears to be a major weakness in the Arizona system of justice, according to Hyder and others, is the imbalance between the state's prosecutorial strengths and the rest of the legal community. In Arizona, they say, there has been a tradition of weak laws and weaker prosecutors. They point out the meager funding for county attorneys and the state attorney general's office has contributed to an inability to provide Arizona with effective prosecution of the more difficult white collar and organized criminal elements.

In addition, the very structure of the judicial system may contribute to the problem.

The Republican majority leader of the state House of Representatives, Burton Barr, tells of his concern about the selection of judges in Arizona. "What disturbs me," says Representative Barr, "is the state Bar Association's role in selecting the judiciary. It would be nice if I could select my boss, well, that's the way we select judges," he commented. "In effect, who a judge will be is decided by the very people who have to go before him," the majority leader explained. "I don't think this is in the best interest of the justice system," he concluded.

Former Republican Congressman Sam Steiger voiced his indictment of the state's legal profession by saying, "The one threat that emerges through all of this is that none of the chicanery could have been possible if it wasn't for the legal profession." Steiger, who was considered an arch-conservative in Washington, said, "One of the problems with Congress is that 62 per cent of its members are lawyers, and believe me—it's a problem."

This controversial and outspoken politician, who was defeated in November 1976 for a seat in the United States Senate, was vehement in his attack on current practices in the legal profession. "I have seen prosecutors, good prosecutors, come down and congratulate a defense attorney for a brilliant legal maneuver that allowed a guilty accused to get off. 'A great piece of work,' " the attorney would say, according to Steiger, "but it wasn't a great piece of work, it violated the basic oath of a lawyer as an officer of the court to defend society first."

In commenting on the inequality between prosecutors and the legal talent available to wealthy and powerful interests, Steiger cited the instance of an old foe, the Emprise Corporation of Buffalo, New York. "Every jurisdiction, including the federal, is outmanned and outgunned by a single entity like that, who can simply afford to employ the best counsel. All prosecutorial jurisdictions have overworked and underexperienced personnel who are literally no match for these kind of people," the former congressman said.

Replying to a question of what can be done, Steiger said, "The answer is not more law, I don't think we should permit the enforcement people to have abusive powers, what it must be is a change in the posture and attitude of lawyers. They have to return to the concept that their first obligation is to society, and then to their client. Their client," he opined, "is only entitled to totally fair treatment, not to subversion of the law." In an aside, Steiger commented, "It's interesting that China, Red China, has the lowest crime rate in the world, and China is also the only so-called civilized country that has outlawed the practice of law."

Problems with Arizona lawyers and members of the state's judiciary were also included in the series of articles written by the group of journalists from the IRE (Investigative Reporters and Editors) who came to the state to investigate crime as a result of the Don Bolles murder.

In Part 23 of the series, the IRE investigators said, "As guardians of the quality of justice in Arizona, judges and lawyers, knowingly or otherwise, have contributed to a permissive atmosphere in which organized crime figures and members of prominent families get lenient treatment, backgrounds of important law-enforcement agents go unchecked, and letters of reference and recommendation flow easily from respectable citizens to questionable acquaintances."

They cited the instance of U. S. District Court Chief Judge Walter E. Craig, a former president of the American Bar Association, who they say causes consternation in prosecutors' offices whenever he is assigned a case involving organized crime. The apprehension, they say, stems from Craig's handling of cases, which reflects "support of the local socio-political power structure and a benign attitude to ward hoodlum defendants."

Judge Craig, the IRE article pointed out, reversed a jury's guilty verdict against Joe Bonanno, Jr., on a conspiracy charge to hire a hit man, and has been extremely lenient to the sons of prominent Arizonans who have been before him on major drug charges.

Judge Craig was quoted by the IRE reporters as saying, "I don't know of any organized crime in Arizona. I hear references made about it, but I don't know who any organized crime figures are. I've read about it, but I've never had any of it in my court."

The new head of the Arizona Bar Association, Phoenix attorney Tom Tang, while not overly worried about the future of crime in Arizona, did admit some shortcomings as alleged by the IRE reporters and others. Tang said, "I have to agree with the IRE series in saying that we have been rather meager in funding proper law-enforcement measures which would be adequate to take into account that kind of a threat. Because it is sophisticated, it is in areas that require more than just the prosecution of individual offenses. From that standpoint," Tang admitted, "you need a Crime Task Force with adequate personnel, and the sophistication to understand what is going on."

When asked to comment on charges that the state Bar Association was "defense-oriented" and negligent in pushing for adequate prosecution, Tang said, "Well, of course, that would be one of those kinds of headline-making charges that would be helpful to prosecution—but, as far as the Bar is concerned, is that really the function of the organized Bar as such?"

County Attorney Hyder, Attorney General Bruce Babbitt, United States Attorney for Arizona Mike Hawkins, and others suggest it is.

Despite the magnificent efforts of individual law-enforcement officers and some dedicated prosecutors, Arizona is not a bad place for criminals.

Former Phoenix City judge Richard Tracey says, "One of the things that has encouraged crime in Arizona is the fact that you have good law of averages in your favor of not getting caught, and the law of averages is increased in your favor by the reason that even if you are caught, because of incompetence, influence, or a number of other unknown factors you can still get away with it."

Discussing white collar crime in particular, Judge Tracey said, "White collar criminals leave all kinds of fingerprints compared to a crime like a burglary, where you've got a whole community and nobody except the criminal knows who took the stolen items. In white collar crime you've got contracts of papers with the criminal's name on it, or somebody else's name, or notarized papers. You've got it all in a package, and all you've got to do is be smart enough to find all your clues," he said.

The major problems in the prosecution of white collar crime, according to Judge Tracey, are overworked prosecutors lacking the necessary facilities and expertness, and an inordinate length of time before such a matter is finally brought to trial. "You see, in most jurisdictions," he said, "the judge watches the case load, and when cases mature to a certain point they are considered ready for trial, but here [Arizona] until the *attorneys* say we are ready to go to trial nobody bothers them." In Arizona, Judge Tracey said, "You can have a twenty- to twenty-five-month delay between the

93

date of the request for the trial and the actual beginning of the trial, whereas, in most systems, the matters are completely out of the system within fifteen months, and seven months is supposed to be the ideal time," he said.

Particularly in the case of white collar and other complex criminal activities Judge Tracey agreed with the proposition that time dilutes crime, and that inordinate delays in both criminal and civil cases are a technique used by members of the legal profession to obviate justice.

Some law-enforcement officers have voiced the opinion that excessive delays in the prosecution of those allegedly involved in the Bolles murder and associated crimes revealed by an investigation into the matter may prevent the achievement of deserved justice.

One Arizona attorney who has served in an elected office says it has been a common practice for lawyers in the state to serve as conduits for the bribing of state officials. He alleged instances when attorneys made payoffs for clients to several people in state government.

In a May 16, 1976, article in the *Arizona Republic*, Walter W. Kerswill, a former official of the Arizona Consumer Loan and Finance Association, was quoted as saying that many Arizona politicians received handouts from an illegal slush fund maintained by his firm. Kerswill said, according to the article, that the money from this slush fund was distributed to the politicians by the Association's "bag man," its legal counsel, attorney Dow Ben Roush.

Though most attorneys would vehemently deny that they ever acted as a conduit for a bribe, there are few who would refuse to act as a messenger boy for a good-paying client and deliver a sealed envelope.

The new United States Attorney for the Arizona district, Mike Hawkins, was asked on a Phoenix television broadcast about the involvement of lawyers with criminal elements in the state, and he answered, "I can't think of a problem that concerns me more, as an individual, than that problem. I'm an attorney, and I'm proud to be an attorney, and I think the fact that I am an attorney in the state of Arizona is a privilege, it is not a license to steal from people, and it is not a license to dream up devious ways to avoid the long arm of the law," Hawkins stated.

"One of the very distressful things I found when I came into this office," he said, "was the extent in numbers that would have exceeded my wildest imagination of lawyer involvement in criminal activity. I think that those of us involved in the prosecution of the law have a special responsibility to address ourselves to that problem," Hawkins commented. "There's a good deal of public suspicion," he offered, "and some of it is well-founded."

"After all," he continued, "in the criminal process, the person that makes the decision to prosecute is a lawyer, the person that makes a decision about the case is a judge, who is a lawyer, and when there is a conviction and it goes up on appeal, the judges who will review the conviction are lawyers. At every step of the procedure lawyers are involved," he said.

"I feel very strongly about attorneys being involved in criminal matters," U. S. Attorney Hawkins emphasized.

A considerable body of public opinion believes that the major problems of crime and corruption in the state of Arizona are the result of law *users*, not law breakers, and they agree with Professor Jerold S. Auerbach in his *Harper's* article, "A Plauge of Lawyers," that "mired in our legalistic swamp, we are easy prey for lawyers." Professor Auerbach said, "The cost of professional legal services puts justice beyond the reach of the poor," and in a statement that fits the

Arizona mold relating to its problems with organized and white collar crime, he said, "Certainly the privileged beneficiaries of the legal culture—primarily the corporations that pay the highest retainer fees—are not clamoring to relinquish their advantages."

It has been suggested that regardless of who pushed the button on the bomb, or who paid to have it done, the real culprit in the murder of Don Bolles was the unholy alliance between big-business interests, politicians, and lawyers.

It is said, particularly by members of the law-enforcement community, that the common practice of seeking and receiving special favors by these interests and a minimal or cosmetic effort to strengthen law enforcement in Arizona have created the atmosphere in which criminal minds could contemplate the murder of a working newsman.

To demonstrate how the unholy alliance operates in Arizona, and how individuals with apparently the best of motives can corrupt a community or a state, it may be well to consider one prime example in which public interests were subverted for private gain, the establishment along the banks of the Colorado River of a community known as Lake Havasu City.

Chapter 6

THE HAVASU CONSPIRACY

Lake Havasu is a body of water created by the damming of the Colorado River near Parker, Arizona. Located approximately 150 miles northwest of Phoenix and 130 miles south of Las Vegas, Lake Havasu is the reservoir from which the metropolitan water districts of Southern California siphon off the waters of the Colorado for use in the sprawling cities of Los Angeles and San Diego. It is a long thin lake stretching 45 miles north from Parker Dam, and about 3 to 4 miles across at its broadest point.

Since the Colorado River forms the boundary between the two states, the western shoreline of Lake Havasu is in California and the eastern shore is a part of Arizona.

The land along this portion of the Lower Colorado is desert country, in which the river has cut through a terrain that varies from flat sandy bottom lands to gentle rolling hills of alluvial gravel, to towering crags of time-worn stone.

It is reached by Arizona State Highway 95 from U.S. 66 to the north and U.S. 10 to the south, and has become a water sports paradise for Southern California and Arizona.

Like Lake Mead, some 125 miles upstream, Lake Havasu is a man-made creation. It had its beginning in

1938 with the completion of Parker Dam, but there was little activity in the vicinity of Lake Havasu proper until 1944 when the Army Air Force built a recuperation center for battle-weary airmen at a place on the Arizona side called Site Six.

Site Six was a flat sandy peninsula that jutted out into the lake nearly two miles. It was ideal for Army Air Force purposes since it could accommodate two 6,500-foot runways on which the recuperating airmen could be flown in and out of the area, yet there was isolation with no paved roads leading to Site Six. To the men who had to fight up in the wild blue yonder, it was a place to get away from it all.

After World War II, it was abandoned by the Air Force and became just an isolated landing strip for sportsmen pilots and a tiny recreation concession for boaters and fishermen who had "off-road" vehicles.

In 1956, the McCulloch Corporation, a blossoming business conglomerate created by Robert McCulloch, bought out the Scott-Atwater Company of Minneapolis, a manufacturer of outboard motors for recreational boats. Headquartered in Los Angeles, McCulloch began a search shortly after the purchase to find a convenient body of water in which to test his boats and motors.

Some testing was done at the Salton Sea south of Palm Springs, California, but the high salt content of the Salton Sea made it unsuitable for the testing of motors that were primarily used in fresh water. McCulloch's engineers tried Lake Mead near Las Vegas, but that too was unsatisfactory. Lake Mead is that vast reservoir created by Hoover Dam, and winds whipping across its broad expanse would churn the surface into large waves that tiny boats and tiny motors couldn't handle. So McCulloch looked elsewhere.

In 1957, he "discovered" Lake Havasu and the old Air Force landing strip, which was more than adequate for use by company planes. It was to be a far-reaching discovery.

In the last half of the 1950s, the Southern California economy took off on the powerful thrust of a newly born Space Age. With aero-space firms and R&D companies leading the way, it was boom time, and highly paid workers had money to spend. Much of it was spent on recreation. On weekends, the freeways leading from the Los Angeles megalopolis were clogged with cars pulling boats and camping trailers to nearby resorts. Anxious to flee the smog and confinement of the city, these weekend vacationers headed for the mountains, the seashore, or wherever they could find a semblance of solitude or outdoor fun.

Land developers and speculators conscious of this escape market began to vie with car dealers and rug merchants for newspaper space or TV time to peddle their recreational properties. Most of this land was nothing more than subdivided parcels of desert. But these developers and speculators weren't selling land, they were selling escape and the promise of tomorrow.

For just a little down and a few dollars a month, anyone could own some land in a planned recreational community. Elaborate brochures and artists' renderings would show how some hunk of desert was to become a "planned" recreational oasis, and of course the ever present "on site" salesman would paint his verbal picture of a glowing future. "Believe me, this is going to become another Palm Springs!" was a common pitch.

One of the top fast-buck land sales organizations at the time was a corporate grouping known under various names as Omart Investment Company, M. Penn Phillips Associates, or Holly Corporation. Located at 1111 West Foothill Boulevard in Azusa, California, it was responsible for sales at the Hesperia development north of San Bernardino, and some projects on the Salton Sea. By 1958, land buyers discovered that fresh water and real potential were not exactly in abundance at Hesperia or the Salton Sea, and as problems began to outweigh the promises, interest in these developments began to wane.

To be a top money-maker, developers and speculators had learned by then, you must have two basic ingredients, cheap land and plenty of fresh water.

The McCulloch conglomerate testing its outboard motors at Site Six was into many things in 1958, manufacturing, oil, and real estate development. So the land development potentials of the Lake Havasu area were not overlooked by the company men riding around in their motorboats. There was certainly plenty of fresh water, and if the land could be had at the right price, it might be a real money-maker.

This same year the National Park Service completed a survey on land uses for the Lower Colorado River. It updated an earlier one made by a subcommittee of the Department of the Interior. These surveys indicated that an increasing number of people were being attracted to the river, and projections on future use were verging on the astronomical. They also called attention to a major problem, squatters. Most of the land from Hoover Dam to the Mexican border was owned and controlled by the federal government, and at many places where there was easy access to the river proper, people were simply taking over the federal lands without permission, building shacks and trailer parks, and preventing public use of the river.

In an area just south of Parker Dam known as the Eleven-mile Strip where some riverfront land was privately owned, the weekend population had jumped from 5,000 persons a day in 1955 to nearly 11,000 persons by 1958, just three years later. Even roadless and remote Lake Havasu jumped from 96,000 visitors in 1950 to 400,000 visitors by 1958. It was clear to government officials that the squatter problem was getting out of hand, and an overall land use plan or zoning of the Lower Colorado was a must.

The McCulloch Corporation, which had purchased the private land that was available, was, as the cliché goes, in the right place at the right time.

Robert P. McCulloch, founder of the company, was born in St. Louis in 1911. His grandfather, John I. Beggs, founded Milwaukee's public utility system, and his father was head of United Railways Company in St. Louis. He attended Princeton in 1928, transferred to Stanford University in 1930, and graduated from the Palo Alto, California, school in 1932 with an engineering degree.

In some ways, his interests and career paralleled those of the late Howard Hughes. He was technically oriented, and in his junior year at Stanford won the Class C and Class D National Outboard Racing championships. When he was twenty, he began to build engines for midget racing cars and started to manufacture superchargers. According to a company biography, his business expanded so rapidly that when he sold it to Borg-Warner in 1943, McCulloch was second only to General Motors in supercharger manufacturing.

He was not a poor boy by any means, and like Hughes he was financially able to develop businesses which matched his interests at the time. During World War II, he founded McCulloch Aviation and embarked on a vast program to develop lightweight engines that would achieve the maximum horsepower per pound. The knowledge acquired was later applied to chain-saw engines, and by 1964, the McCulloch Corporation was the world's largest manufacturer of chain saws and the third largest producer in the world of outboard motors.

McCulloch's interests were by no means limited to things technical. Prior to the venture into Arizona, a McCulloch news release said that Robert had developed the Thunderbird Valley Estates in Palm

101

Springs, the Lake Mead Marina, and the world's largest floating restaurant on Lake Mead. At the time he was also publisher of a monthly magazine, *Palm Springs Life*, and the president of the annual Palm Springs Golf Classic.

In his company biography, Bob McCulloch is described as a relaxed and casual man whose energy and drive seem to belie his easygoing exterior. "He is so open-handed with his competitors that he takes them on tours of his plants, shows them his latest tricks—and still reckons on staying several jumps ahead of them," the biography says.

Grandiose and flamboyant in his business concepts, he liked to surround himself with assistants of a similar nature.

One such assistant who became his right arm in the development of Lake Havasu City and other projects was an industrial engineer and planner, C. V. Wood, Jr. Wood was born in Wood County, Oklahoma, in 1920. He attended Hardin-Simmons and after two years transferred to Oklahoma University, where he received a bachelor's degree in petroleum engineering in 1941.

Soon after graduation he joined Convair, an aircraft-manufacturing firm, and wound up as Convair's chief industrial engineer at the ripe old age of twenty-eight. In 1950, he became director of Southern California activities of the prestigious Stanford Research Institute, heading up techno-economics research projects for industry and the federal government, according to a McCulloch release. Wood stayed with SRI until 1954, when he became the very first person to be hired by Disneyland, Inc. As vice-president and general manager, he supervised selection and purchase of the land as well as the design, engineering, and construction of the Disneyland project.

It was during the construction phase that Wood first met Robert McCulloch.

McCulloch was visiting the Disneyland site, and Wood, who had hurt his knee in an accident, was on crutches. "It was a bitch getting around that place," he remarked in an interview. McCulloch, who was tooling up to manufacture electric golf carts at the time, noticed Wood's discomfort. "Would you like to have one of my carts to test?" he asked, and Wood eagerly responded, "Man! Mr. McCulloch, there's nothing I'd like more."

From this golf cart incident at the Disneyland construction site sprang a real friendship, Wood recalled. The friendship ripened into business partnerships in such projects as the huge amusement center on the beach near Santa Monica, California, known as Pacific Ocean Park, and eventually the planned community on the Lower Colorado named Lake Havasu City.

Disneyland opened in July of 1955 at Anaheim, California, near Los Angeles, and C. V. Wood, Jr., stayed on as general manager for a year. In 1956, however, he left Disneyland to form his own collection of companies known as the Marco Engineering Group, and set up business to build various amusement parks and other projects around the world.

Both C. V. Wood, Jr., and Robert McCulloch were imaginative "large project" entrepreneurs. If a philosophical label could be slapped on their combined careers it would be the simple phrase "Think Big!"

For a period of time their business relationship was spasmodic.

It was during this period that McCulloch purchased Scott-Atwater, looked for outboard testing sites, and eventually settled on Lake Havasu.

According to C. V. Wood, Jr., McCulloch was sufficiently interested in the Lake Havasu area by late March of 1958 that he landed at the Site Six airstrip to begin negotiations on the purchase of the available private land. About 3,500 acres, including a 40-acre parcel on the Site Six peninsula itself, were available in the Havasu area. Most of the acreage was full sections (640 acres per section) interspersed in checkboard fashion between sections of federally owned and controlled land.

McCulloch was able to persuade the owners to sell at a price described as fair, and he was able to arrange a long-term lease with the U. S. Bureau of Fish and Wildlife for another 1,000 acres deemed necessary for his plans.

Most of the private land he purchased had no access to the lake itself, so it seems apparent that the testing of outboard motors was not all he had in mind when he made the purchases. It was rugged desert land he bought, of little apparent value at the time. But so was Palm Springs before its buildings and golf courses!

What this purchase of land and long-term lease of federal property accomplished was to give the McCulloch Corporation a vested interest in the Lake Havasu area and the cosmetic clout necessary to get state and federal assistance to build roads and develop this potentially excellent recreational region.

In the comparatively crude and often naïve economic climate of Arizona in the late 1950s, it was clearly evident that the state's politicians and business leaders were hooked on a narcotic called growth. Echoes of the California boom were resounding through the halls of the state Capitol and Arizona's financial institutions, and the leadership of its establishment was eager for its piece of the action. The Del Webb Corporation was putting the finishing touches to a planned retirement community just west of Phoenix called Sun City, and a posh Western-style suburb known as Scottsdale was acquiring a national reputation. Growth was the panacea to cure the ills of a bucolic economy.

The problem with being hooked on any narcotic is that the craving can overwhelm a person's common sense to a point where he will do just about anything to get a fix. So it was with growth and Arizona's leadership.

When the McCulloch Corporation began to evidence an interest in the state, the powers that be were more than willing to cooperate.

After Robert McCulloch acquired the land and federal lease arrangement at Lake Havasu for an outboard testing facility, he began to think in terms of developing what he had as a modest recreational resort. This nominal concept exploded into a full-fledged idea for a brand-new "planned community" as the result of a city council decision in Los Angeles, California.

C. V. Wood, Jr., who is currently chairman of the board of McCulloch Oil Corporation, explains what happened. "Bob McCulloch had some land near the new Los Angeles airport where his factory was located, and one day, all of a sudden, his phone is ringing and people are wanting to buy his land. Suddenly that land was worth $250,000 an acre," Wood continued, "and he couldn't figure out the reason why. Well, the reason was," Wood explained, "that the zoning had been changed so you could build a thirteen-story hotel there. Before the height limitation had been something like thirty feet."

McCulloch's factory occupied about 20 acres on the 60 acres of land he owned near the airport, and the sudden increase in land value made it more profitable to sell the land rather than maintaining his factory at the location. So he began to look elsewhere for a factory site. By 1959, McCulloch had decided that the Lake Havasu area might make a good location for his manufacturing operations despite its relative isolation.

He then called on his friend, C. V. Wood, Jr., for an evaluation. Wood, after looking at the site, told McCulloch in some choice language that he didn't think the suggested project was feasible.

Wood in an interview tells what happened. "I knew he had his heart set on it, so I said, 'Tell you what, Bob. I'll have my research economists do a little quick and dirty study on this thing, just to prove it's hopeless.' In a couple of months my guys finished the study," Wood continued. "I'll be gosh-darned, when I saw that thing I said, 'I can't believe this! If we can make a bunch of pieces go together, this is a perfect site for a new community.' "

Wood explained that the project was possible, but only if McCulloch would move at least five hundred workers over there to furnish an economic base. McCulloch agreed, and Wood then joined the team and merged his Marco Engineering Group with McCulloch.

In conversations with top executives of large successful corporations, one can often be misled into a belief that major decisions are just the intuitive whims of bold enterprising men and women. This of course is nonsense! When millions of dollars are invested, it is a calculated risk based on reliable information and research. Many questions must be answered before any successful corporation will plow its funds into a new venture. Lake Havasu was no exception.

To have a manufacturing plant you must have employees, and if you have employees you must have a community nearby in which they can live. At Lake Havasu, there was nothing within a reasonable distance to fit this description. Which meant Robert McCulloch was viewing the area with an idea of building a brand-new community prior to his 1959 conversation with C. V. Wood, Jr.

Since the land he had purchased was scattered throughout the Havasu area, intermixed with various federal and state lands, he had to have some reasonable assurance that these governmental lands would be made available for his commercial purposes. He also had to have some reasonable assurance that roads would be built leading to the area or he couldn't have considered the idea in the first place. Obviously, these assurances had to come from government officials, both state and federal, who controlled the land in question.

Just when McCulloch put out his first feelers is somewhat obscure, but it must have been early in the game. Apparently McCulloch determined that in order to make the venture feasible, the company would have to acquire an additional 13,000 acres of surrounding land from the government. To make this acquisition possible, it was necessary for the company to know:

1. What government agency controlled the land?

2. Could they sell the land to a single private interest?

3. How could such a sale be consummated?

4. How much help could be expected from the state of Arizona to acquire roads and other public facilities?

5. How much assistance would be provided by Mohave County, Arizona?

6. Was it possible to install the necessary public utilities such as water, electricity, and telephones?

7. How much would it cost the company (McCulloch) in total?

The answers to these questions were not received overnight.

The McCulloch organization undoubtedly contacted the Federal Bureau of Land Management, the Bureau of Reclamation, the Bureau of Fish and Wildlife, the Arizona Land Department, the Arizona Highway Department, the Mohave County Board of Supervisors, and various other federal, state, and county agencies to get the answers.

An organization willing to probe the conditions, attitudes, and situations of the time would have learned that studies by various federal agencies from 1950

107

through 1958 had created a sense of urgency to clean up the many problems which were making the Lower Colorado from Davis Dam to the south nearly uncontrollable. In essence, these agencies were advocating a crash program for land use or zoning on the Lower Colorado.

Pressures from within these agencies to justify their increasing budgets, and pressures from politicians, real estate promoters, environmentalists, and other outside sources had created an atmosphere of crisis.

McCulloch knew that a federal blessing to urbanize the area was the first step in acquiring the federal land he wanted. Whether by intent or circumstance, McCulloch's first approaches to these government agencies emphasized the public recreational aspects in the development of Lake Havasu. This approach fit neatly into governmental plans for the area.

As often occurs with crash programs, the urgency to achieve an objective will cause its participants to view the situation with tunnel vision. Expediency becomes the order of the day, and careful analysis goes by the boards. Something had to be done quickly to solve the problem of squatters who had grabbed federal lands illegally. Any proposal that offered an orderly approach to public use of the river was welcome, and McCulloch's plans were a quick and ready solution for the Lake Havasu portion of the Lower Colorado.

So when the McCulloch Corporation advanced the idea of acquiring some 13,000 acres of government land, it seemed like a good idea, similar to the idea expressed in the comment attributed to former Defense Secretary Charles Wilson, "What's good for General Motors is good for America." The majority of those involved setting up the land purchase seemed to think, "What's good for the McCulloch Corporation is good for Arizona and the Lower Colorado Basin."

On April 13, 1960, an article appeared in the *Ari-*

zona Republic stating, "The McCulloch Corp., a nationally known firm manufacturing chain saws, marine engines, and water craft, may build a plant in Arizona in expanding its operations, it was suggested yesterday. The possibility was mentioned in a conference during which the firm asked the state Highway Commission to help provide access roads to a public recreation area it is developing along the shores of Lake Havasu."

It was also mentioned in the article that the recreational facility would cost some 11 million over the next seven years and that McCulloch officials said that $750,000 had already been spent in the area by the company. Nothing was mentioned in the article indicating that a city or homesites would be built.

This was probably one of the first public utterances on the McCulloch Corporation's plans for Lake Havasu, but the behind-the-scenes work had been under way for some time.

What's so wrong with private enterprise developing a new community in the desert along the Colorado? it might be asked.

The answer is simple. It's not what was done that's wrong, it's how it was done.

Among the cast of characters who played a role in the Havasu conspiracy was a New Mexico attorney-legislator from Silver City by the name of Charles Royall.

In 1959, sometime after McCulloch discovered Havasu, Royall left New Mexico to take a job as a deputy attorney general in Arizona. He joined the staff of Attorney General Wade Church and was immediately assigned as the legal adviser to Arizona Land Commissioner Obed Lassen. He wasn't the ordinary run-of-the-mill lawyer who works in the AG's office, he was a land specialist, and powerful members of the Arizona Legislature let the then attorney general know that Royall was to be the land commissioner's attorney and nothing else.

In response to a question whether he knew Charles Royall prior to his arrival in Arizona, C. V. Wood, Jr., then head of McCulloch Oil, said, "No, I didn't know him, but I can't speak for other members of my staff." The importance of this question will be revealed later in the chapter.

Royall, however, was something special, and from 1959 through 1963 was the one and only legal adviser to the Arizona Land Department.

Another attorney who joined the Arizona attorney general's staff in 1959 was Neal Roberts, whose name was to surface in the investigation of the Don Bolles murder. He also would acquire some financial interests at Lake Havasu City.

It was Charles Royall, however, who found his castle keep on the Colorado, as payment for services rendered.

The state land commissioner at the time, Obed Lassen, could be described as one of Arizona's "good old boys." Loyal as hell to the conservative leadership of the state, Lassen and Royall were destined to do the ground work in piecing together the Havasu plot for McCulloch.

These were the state officials who theoretically were the guardians of state-owned lands for the schoolchildren of Arizona, to whom the lands were given by federal government through the Enabling Act of 1912.

The state of Arizona has a total land area of 72,688,000 acres. Out of this total the federal government owns, controls, and manages about 71 per cent of all lands in the state. The state government owns or holds in trust approximately 13 per cent and the remainder, approximately 16 per cent, is deeded and private land.

As a result of the Enabling Act of 1912, the state of Arizona was given the authority to select from federal lands not specifically withdrawn for public purposes a large amount of acreage at no cost. The state could then either lease or sell this land with the revenues going into a trust fund for the state's schools.

In 1960, the state of Arizona had 734,813 acres of this trust land remaining in its land bank account with the federal government.

As the guardian of state-owned land, and the trustee of the land bank account with the federal government, it was the duty of the state Land Department to look after the interest of the people of Arizona, and in the case of the trust account, the schoolchildren of the state. When state lands were sold, the duty of the state land commissioner was to make certain that the state would receive the best possible price for its property, and when selecting available federal land for the school trust, to make sure that the best and most valuable lands were selected for the school trust fund.

McCulloch discovered early in his investigation that the only way his company could acquire the 13,000 acres he desired at Lake Havasu was to have the state of Arizona select this acreage from the government by using its land bank account (the trust lands). Then, once the state had acquired the title to the land, it could sell the property to his firm under the laws of the state.

While the U. S. Bureau of Land Management (BLM) theoretically could have sold some of the land directly to McCulloch, federal law limits the amount it is possible to sell to a single individual or corporation. That amount is 700 acres. McCulloch felt that 13,000 acres was necessary to a reasonably profitable venture, so the state of Arizona was chosen to be the middleman in order to get around the acreage limitation.

The state of Arizona also had limits on the amount of land that could be sold to a single individual or corporation. 160 acres was maximum for agricultural

111

lands, and 640 acres for grazing lands, which was considered the acreage of lowest value owned by the state.

However, there was a loophole.

In Arizona law, commercial land, which traditionally had the highest valuation, had no acreage limitation. This loophole became the conduit by which the Havasu conspiracy was able to deliver the 13,000 acres of public land into the hands of one single private interest.

Never in the history of the state prior to the sale to the McCulloch Corporation, and never since, was a land parcel of this size sold to a single group or person. And it demonstrated to the business community, ethical and unethical, that both the federal government and the state of Arizona could be used for private gain.

For the McCulloch Corporation to proceed with its plans for Lake Havasu, it was necessary to know at an early stage that the state of Arizona would request the 13,000 acres from the U.S. government, and that this land would then be resold in one single large package by the state to McCulloch. They had to know if the state Land Department not only would do the enormous amount of work necessary to get the land, but was willing to take the unprecedented step to classify the land commercial, sell it at a bargain price, and set up the sale in such a fashion that it would be legal but only the McCulloch Corporation could as a practical matter buy it.

Needless to say, the required assurances were given.

Who, at the time, could possibly give such assurances?

In varying degrees, the participants in the Havasu conspiracy had to include: Governor Paul Fannin (later U.S. senator), state Land Commissioner Obed Lassen, state Attorney General Robert Pickrell, the leadership of the Arizona Legislature, plus the lawyers, bankers, and businessmen who form the controlling elements of the Arizona establishment. In addition, cooperation was necessary from the Secretary of the Interior and the members of the Arizona congressional delegation. Without the assistance of the aforementioned, the sale of the land to McCulloch would have been impossible!

While some of those involved may have had greater culpability than others, all who knew and condoned this huge sale of public land to one single private interest served the cause of white collar crime.

Primary concern for the interests of the public in general is the essential bond, the glue, that holds a nation together. Just to survive, the needs and desires of private interests must be a secondary consideration. The persons who took part in the Havasu conspiracy did not subscribe to such an opinion.

When the McCulloch Corporation met with the Arizona Highway Commission in April of 1960 to get public funds to build public roads for a private interest, one of the highway commissioners was a former state senator, Frank L. Christensen from Flagstaff. Christensen was one of many who did the spadework for McCulloch in the early days.

According to the current head of McCulloch Oil, C. V. Wood, Jr., "The first man we worked with was a fellow named Frank from Flagstaff. He had something to do with the state Highway Commission," Wood explained in an interview, "and he worked with us for about a year. When he got sick," Wood continued, "and couldn't do it any longer, he said we ought to get ahold of Harold Giss to help us out. After Frank died, we hired Giss," Wood explained.

Ex-Senator Frank Christensen died on June 30, 1962. One year later, on August 2, 1963, the 13,000 acres of public land were sold by the state of Arizona to McCulloch.

Harold Giss, a state senator from Yuma, Arizona, was known at the time as the most powerful man in the

Arizona Legislature, and undoubtedly was the chief ramrod in making the sale possible.

A short, corpulent man, Giss was to the Arizona Senate what Lyndon Johnson was to the U. S. Senate. A Democrat, he served both as majority and minority leader, according to the fortunes of politics. Like Johnson, he had an extraordinary ability in legislative leadership, and could buttonhole, cajole, threaten, and convince fellow members of the Legislature to do most anything he felt necessary for the state.

His public image exuded warmth and concern for his constituents, and year after year the voters of Yuma County elected him to office. To the electorate, he was also the political bulwark who fought their battles against the big distant cities of Phoenix and Tucson.

Yuma, Arizona, is located on the banks of the Colorado River near the Mexican border, and is actually closer to San Diego, California, than it is to the Arizona capital at Phoenix.

Though he was a major participant in the Havasu conspiracy, he was also a dedicated and effective legislator for sparsely populated Yuma County, and it would not be fair or factual to label him as a villain. Giss was Giss, a composite of virtues and vices whose basic problem was an excessive enjoyment of power.

While it is true that he was on McCulloch's payroll as a consultant, at an annual salary of $6,600 in 1965, it is doubtful to those who knew him that this relatively small consultant's fee was the major factor in his strenuous efforts to get the Lake Havasu land for McCulloch. Most knowledgeable Arizonans are certain that he genuinely believed the project was good for the state.

Despite the contention of some that he was "bought," this seems unlikely, since he filed for bankruptcy on April 17, 1966, while he was still a powerful figure in politics.

His unique position in the Arizona Senate could

have furnished the basis for vast amounts of graft, but there is little evidence to suggest he profited financially.

To illustrate his enormous influence, it was often said, "The Arizona Legislature is a body of men surrounded by Harold Giss."

On April 20, 1961, President Kennedy's new Secretary of the Interior, Stewart Udall, an Arizonan, announced a solution to the problems plaguing the Lower Colorado River area. The Secretary's announcement contained two principal actions, establishment of an application and permit plan (for squatters) and the preparation of a comprehensive land use plan.

On June 7, 1961, Secretary Udall announced the appointment of the Lower Colorado River Land Use Advisory Committee, to be made up of representatives of the governors of the states involved, as well as representatives of each county and political area along the river. According to the published report of this committee, it was set up to evaluate and advise the Secretary on the practicability of the many and varied requests from a wide variety of interests along the river.

On June 8, 1961, Arizona State Senator Harold C. Giss was elected chairman of the committee. It also included: Obed Lassen, Arizona state land commissioner; Senator Robert E. Morrow, Mohave County, Arizona; Ray J. Nesbitt, representing California Governor Edmund Brown; Robert Nissen, Yuma County board of supervisors; Ross Dana, San Bernardino County, California; A. J. Shaver, representing Governor Sawyer of Nevada; William Claypool III of Needles, California; Samuel Haydis of Salome, Arizona; Harry A. Hunt of Imperial County, California; and LeRoy Kamrar of Blythe, California.

With a committee such as this, in retrospect it could be said the fox was in the henhouse. In reality, however, the fox had been a resident of the henhouse for at least two or three years.

Aided and abetted by Governor Fannin, Land Commissioner Lassen, Charles Royall, and various federal bureaucrats, Harold Giss was in an excellent position to steer urban development along the Lower Colorado. The Department of the Interior and other federal agencies involved didn't want state and local hassles to slow down its zoning of the river, and the advisory committee was the method chosen to get local and regional input and blessing for the overall land use plan.

By mid-1962, the Havasu conspiracy was in high gear.

In Phoenix, the state Land Department was busy putting together the necessary paper work to get the land McCulloch wanted from the federal government.

In Washington, the federal agencies were busy ironing out the bureaucratic details necessary to the transfer.

At El Centro and Apple Valley, California, the representatives of the McCulloch Corporation were meeting with federal officials and the Lower Colorado River Land Use Advisory Committee to smooth out any technical problems.

Nowhere did anyone of consequence suggest that there might be other possibilities for the use of the Lake Havasu land.

No one said, "Hey, wait a minute! There might be other developers who would be interested in Havasu."

In a nation that prides itself on a competitive free-enterprise economic system, both state and federal officials were setting up the deal for a single favored private interest. Before the land was even transferred to the state of Arizona for resale at "public auction," it was a foregone conclusion that the land would be sold to McCulloch. As testimony to this allegation is the

116

following letter from Secretary of the Interior Stewart Udall to U.S. Senator Carl Hayden:

Dear Senator Hayden:

This is in further reply to your letters of August 17, October 11, and November 20, 1962, relative to the interest of the McCulloch Properties, Incorporated, in obtaining certain lands in Arizona on which it desires to develop manufacturing, research, and recreation facilities.

In reviewing the overall land needs of the various agencies of the Interior Department in connection with the Lower Colorado River Land Use Program, it was determined that certain lands under withdrawal by the Bureau of Reclamation and the Fish and Wildlife Service, which were of interest to the McCulloch Properties, Incorporated, could be relinquished and returned to the Bureau of Land Management. We are pleased to advise you that both of these Agencies have relinquished their interest in these lands and restoration orders are being processed. Negotiations with the McCulloch Properties, Incorporated, will proceed under the land laws administered by the Bureau of Land Management.

The enclosures transmitted with your letter of August 17 are returned as requested.

Sincerely yours,
Stewart L. Udall
Secretary of the Interior

State Senator Harold Giss was also in communication with Washington, as evidenced by the following letter to Joseph A. Ferstl, Jr., secretary to Carl Hayden:

Dear Friend:

The telegram you sent concerning the action of the Interior Department about the lands in the Site Six area in Mohave County is deeply appreciated. I am prompted to write this personal note to you since the last statement in the telegram must have my comment. The statement reads: "It is hoped that Senator Hayden has been of some assistance in this matter."

Joe, we in Arizona know how the job gets done, who does it, and the prestige of the name of Senator Carl Hayden. Those of us who work in the public interest would be lost on the many pathways of attempting to do things if it were not for the high road that leads to Senator Hayden and his fine office.

Please accept this letter in the highest complimentary manner and be certain that every effort from your end is most deeply appreciated.

With best wishes and kindest regards to you and all at the office, I am

Sincerely,
Harold C. Giss

These were but a few of the communications flitting between Phoenix and Washington on the matter.

It is interesting that in the correspondence and news stories of the period, the planned community and real estate development aspect of the McCulloch plan was seldom, if ever, mentioned.

In the Interior Department's published report, "The Lower Colorado River Land Use Plan," McCulloch's activities were described as following: "The McCulloch Corp. is developing plans for an urban-research-educational-recreation concession complex at Site Six on private land near Lake Havasu." Other than the word "urban," there was no suggestion to indicate the subdivided land sales use. The basic pitch at the time was a manufacturing plant for the state and a big-time recreational facility for the public.

While political pressures on the Department of the Interior were great, the McCulloch Corporation did some arm-twisting of its own. In a letter to Graham Hollister, a special assistant to Secretary Udall, dated August 8, 1962, C. V. Wood, Jr., executive vice-president of McCulloch Properties, Inc., said, "However, if we cannot have some reasonable assurance, within the next few weeks, that we will be able to purchase the land [through the state sale] prior to the end of the year, we find ourselves in the position of definitely having to revert to the other site selection, in California, so that we can assure our ability to meet our present and future production schedules."

By July of 1963, all the details of the land transfer were complete, and the state Land Department announced the proposed sale to McCulloch.

To the public it was a rather stunning announcement, and soon, some bewildered opponents surfaced. One such group was the Arizona Conservation Council, whose Public Land Committee met with Lewis Duncan, deputy land commissioner, to find out why.

Duncan reportedly said that private development of the area was recommended by the Lower Colorado River Land Use Committee. He admitted that it was done "at the request of the McCulloch Company, a California firm, which wants to purchase the land."

After talking with Duncan, the committee requested a full meeting of the Council to consider the action. They listed the following reasons:

1. Sale of the 13,000 acres in one block as proposed is not in the public interest because the block is so large that the highest price will not be obtained.

2. Sale of the land in such a large block violates the intent of the state constitution and the Enabling Act.

3. The acquisition of the land from the federal government for the admitted purpose of selling it to the McCulloch firm violates the intent of the Enabling Act and is not in the best interests of the state.

4. Sale of the land before the new highway reaches the area is not in the public interest because it would be appraised at a much higher figure when it becomes easily accessible for homesites.

The committee had learned from Duncan that the land had been appraised by only one appraiser at an average price of $75 per acre, or a total of $954,329.

McCulloch's powerful proponents came forward to defend the sale.

Harold Giss spoke to the Arizona Conservation Council and told them his Land Use Committee was backing McCulloch's plan. "As soon as we discovered that this plan was compatible with the Interior Department's land use program we so advised the Secretary," he said.

Charles Royall, assistant attorney general assigned to the State Land Department, rose to the occasion, and in a front-page story lauded the sale as "fully justified." Royall told the *Phoenix Gazette*, "The McCulloch firm not only proposes to put the land on tax rolls but expects immediately to create a city of 28,000 industrial employees, providing full recreational facilities for families. He said the area has a capacity for a city of 50,000 and could grow into a community of that size. This will mean not only taxes from the land itself, but sales taxes and other benefits for that area and the state," Royall said.

Meanwhile, the Arizona State Parks Board requested 800 acres of Lake Havasu land be set aside for public park use.

After considerable behind-the-scenes pressure, the Arizona Conservation Council voted 7 to 4 not to oppose the sale.

The request for public recreational land by the State Parks Board was turned down by Land Commissioner Obed Lassen, and the date was set for public auction, August 2, 1963, on the steps of the courthouse at the Mohave County seat at Kingman, Arizona.

Anyone with $954,329.30 in his pocket who was willing to go along with McCulloch's proposal could bid on the 13,000 acres of public land. Oddly enough, on August 2 no one except a McCulloch representative showed up to bid.

The deed was done, and McCulloch paid $73.47 per acre for the largest single tract of state land ever sold.

Despite the raw-land propaganda of the time, and since, the $73 per acre price was a rip-off of extraordinary proportions, based on land sale valuation of the time.

In the four years preceding this sale, the average price paid for an acre of state land was $369.65, and the average price paid for state land in the four years after the sale was $218.40. During the same year as the McCulloch sale, 1963, state grazing land sold for $186.65 per acre.

In 1963, at the Eleven-mile Strip immediately south of Lake Havasu, riverfront properties were selling for $100 to $200 per frontage foot.

Even Obed Lassen in his final report as state land commissioner boasted that in his thirteen-year tenure the average price paid for state land was $256.86 per acre.

"Why," some asked at the time, "didn't the state select for the school trust federal lands in areas of the state where acre lots were selling for $795 per acre and up?"

Six months later, McCulloch Properties announced that homes were going up at the rate of two a week on the 12,000 acres which would be used for "residential" purposes. Lot prices, it was announced, would start at

$2,390. Conservatively assuming half-acre lots, this would mean a gross potential on residential land alone was $57,360,000.

Thus the raw-land façade fell away to reveal the real estate gold therein. The Havasu conspiracy had succeeded.

Chapter 7

BOUGHT AND SOLD

Even prior to the sale of the public lands to McCulloch, the company was busy organizing the sales and operational structure for Lake Havasu City. Every avenue that could make the venture more profitable was explored, and when the sale was completed the McCulloch organization was ready.

First, however, it was payoff time for some of those involved with the conspiracy that made it possible.

Senator Giss continued on the McCulloch payroll as a consultant, and McCulloch hired a law firm from Giss's power base, Yuma, Arizona, to set up the municipal structure for the projected Lake Havasu City. Assisted by McCulloch's own legal adviser, Robert G. Krechter, the Yuma firm of Westover, Copple, Keddie, and Choules was chosen to create some kind of municipal government by which the developer could maintain control of a growing community, minimize state and federal taxes to the developer, and place the burden of municipal facilities on future owners of the land.

Charles Royall, who did such a magnificent job in setting up the purchase for McCulloch while in his official position of deputy attorney general in the Land Department, did not go unrecognized. C. V. Wood, Jr., said in an interview that he contacted Land Commissioner Obed Lassen and asked if he could hire Royall. "I told Lassen I'd like to hire Royall but I didn't want to make it tough on the Land Department in trying to get a replacement," he said. "Lassen said it was alright, so we hired him."

Neither Wood nor Lassen nor Royall could see any "conflict of interest" in this action, apparently. Wood didn't mention just "when" he talked to Lassen about hiring Royall, or when he first talked to Royall himself about employment with McCulloch.

As mentioned in the previous chapter, Wood denied having known Royall prior to his moving to Arizona, but could not speak for other members of his staff.

Whether Royall was actually placed in the Land Department through McCulloch pressure or merely came to the company's attention during the negotiations for the 13,000 acres of public land remains an unconfirmed mystery. It is admitted, however, that a sufficient rapport was established between Royall and the McCulloch interests that Deputy Attorney General Charles Royall was offered the job of chief administrative officer, the city manager, so to speak, of Lake Havasu City.

On December 25, 1963, five months after completion of the land sale, Charles Royall formally announced his resignation from the state Land Department to take over as the administrative head of McCulloch's planned community.

Meanwhile, upstream at the site of the future Lake Havasu City, workmen were busy, and from McCulloch's publicity releases it was learned that in a matter of six months this desert wasteland was being transformed into a metropolis. From news releases dated February 6, 1964, Robert McCulloch was quoted as saying, "Lake Havasu City is now an under-construction reality."

C. V. Wood, Jr., then vice-president of McCulloch

Properties, Inc., listed a number of operations as nearing completion or soon to start:

    . . . paving 31 miles of city roads and streets, of which 10 miles of surfacing is complete.

    . . . public utilities—power, water, and telephone systems have been installed.

    . . . the first bungalow units of the 200-room Lake Havasu hotel, and its public rooms, including a restaurant and cocktail lounge, will be completed by February 15.

    . . . construction of Unit No. 1 of the McCulloch Corporation factory complex is under way. Engine components will be assembled at this plant. The McCulloch Corporation will concentrate future production expansion at Lake Havasu City.

    . . . a 32-unit apartment house will be completed in March, although its first tenants are moving in within two weeks. Site clearing is under way for additional apartment units.

    . . . construction of a shopping center and commercial area has started. (The Valley National Bank, Arizona's No. 1 financial institution, the Phoenix Title and Trust Company, and Claypool's Markets, the Colorado River area's top retailing chain, have contracted for space in the center.)

    . . . immediate development and improvement of the 23-mile-long beachfront, where 1,080 acres are under lease from the Federal Government, as a national watersports area and sportsmen's playground. Thousands of tons of golden sand are being trucked in to cushion bathing beaches.

    . . . completion of the Nautical Inn next month will increase lodging accommodations available for visitors. The inn's dining room and bar, with a capacity of 180 patrons, and a marine store will be completed next month.

. . . the first homes are going up at the rate of two a week on the 12,000 acres which will be used for residential purposes. Homes at Lake Havasu will be priced from $12,500, and lot prices start at $2,390.

All of this had been accomplished in six months!

Amazing, since this had supposedly been raw desert without a virtue in the world.

But there were more amazing things revealed in the McCulloch news releases:

"Exhaustive surveys of many cities and undeveloped locales were made before the Lake Havasu area was chosen as the best available site in the United States for a project of this nature and scope. Over $100,000 was spent on these surveys alone. Among the key factors instrumental in Havasu's selection were its proximity to transportation (U.S. Highway 66 and the Santa Fe main line are 18 miles to the north), a copious water supply (five wells drilled on the townsite already provide enough water for industrial and domestic needs of a city of 15,000 people), and its super-clement weather (the southwest quarter of Arizona is the sunniest in the U.S.)."

Another press release quote: "With its ever-growing accessibility, the city is open to no charges that it will be 'in the middle of nowhere'; it will be no more remote than Phoenix or Yuma is 'remote.' All-weather State Highway 95, *recently completed*, runs north to U.S. 66. A 22-mile highway, running south to the town of Parker, will link the city with U.S. 60 and 70; on this stretch, bulldozers have already pushed through the completed survey road."

A truly fantastic accomplishment, since only six

months earlier it was reported that the land was only accessible by a rough, winding desert road from Topock, though it was admitted that a highway was under construction.

In a statement that summed up a description of the Lake Havasu City project, the McCulloch press release said, "The projected city has been aptly described as Palm Springs *with water*. It will be a far cry from just another desert land development (the Havasu land is arid but very fertile) or a speculator's dream."

The company in its February 1964 press kit also outlined some of its land sales techniques, and corporate promises to bring its manufacturing facilities to the area.

According to the press release, "Perhaps uniquely in the history of U.S. real estate operations of this magnitude, *no land in Lake Havasu City, either residential or commercial, will be sold sight unseen*. In addition, *free transportation*, chiefly by air, will be provided for prospective buyers from many cities west of the Mississippi. Indeed, if a sufficient number of buyers from New York City, for example, display an interest in Havasu ownership, wings will be provided for them from even that far away. McCulloch Properties, Inc., itself has laid down the rule requiring purchaser's onsite inspections of the property. It is not required by Arizona state law."

As to McCulloch's industrial commitment, the press release said, "The future of Lake Havasu City, moreover, is solidly guaranteed by another factor of tremendous weight: *McCulloch Corp. intends to concentrate its future plant expansion in the area*. The company now has some 4,000 employees; its work force is growing at a rate of eight percent a year. Thus, the company foresees a 1,000-employee contingent at Lake Havasu City by 1968, and 4,000 employees there—doubling its present work force—by 1975. This means, if due allowance is made for families and supporting commercial services, *the city should boast a population of no less than 28,000 only twelve years hence*, based on standard U. S. Chamber of Commerce payroll-population ratios. This projection—note carefully—includes no new residents of Lake Havasu City coming from any other sources. It ignores the fact that the area is bound to attract thousands of residents having no connection with McCulloch Corp. but coming there to support the leisure industry that is certain to develop."

The basic impression conveyed to the public at the time was McCulloch's intense desire to move his manufacturing facilities to Lake Havasu, and the real estate development aspect was merely an adjunct to furnish the facilities to attract and hold potential employees.

Governor Fannin expressed this view in his welcoming letter dated February 6, 1964.

> *I am happy to extend a warm welcome to Robert P. McCulloch and his associates. They are building Lake Havasu City and an industrial complex on a foundation of raw desert along the Colorado River and the mid-western border area of Arizona.*
>
> *This is a pioneering enterprise in the best western tradition which the people of Arizona know and understand because it is their own heritage. Arizona needs more projects that will tie manufacturing facilities to city development of the type now under way at Lake Havasu City so more jobs can be available for our widely diversified work force.*
>
> *Like many others in Arizona who have financed and developed similar projects, I congratulate Mr. McCulloch and those working*

128

> *toward the fulfillment of their goal at Lake Havasu.*
>
> Paul Fannin
> Governor

C. V. Wood, Jr., of McCulloch Oil, quoted in a recent interview, said, "Oddly enough, Bob's [McCulloch] idea in Havasu was never to make money on land, but to find a new home for his factory."

Perhaps this was true, but the high-powered sales organization that was set up seems to have indicated a more than casual concern with real estate sales.

One of the pioneers in desert land sales in California was M. Penn Phillips, who was involved in the early days at Palm Springs and later in Hesperia, near the Salton Sea, and other locales. Phillips and his associates were interconnected with a polyglot of corporations all headquartered at 1111 West Foothill Boulevard, Azusa, California, in the late 1950s. Among this polyglot of corporate structures was Omart Investment Company and the Holly Corporation.

The Holly Corporation in turn was parent to a group of subsidiaries and divisions such as: Hesperia Construction Company, Hesperia Golf and Country Club, Hesperia Inn, Hesperia Museum, Hesperia Recreation Club, Hesperia Sales Company, Holly Development Company, Salton Home Builders, Inc., Salton Industrial Development Company, Salton Riviera, Inc., Salton Vista Development Company, and The Mount Vernon Company.

If anyone could sell the proverbial refrigerator to the Eskimos it was Holly Corporation. They had a corps of sales representatives trained in the deserts of Southern California, hardened in battle with the eager dream buyers of the Los Angeles metroplex, and with the scruples necessary to do most any sales job.

The Holly reputation was undoubtedly known to

Robert McCulloch, since the firm or firms associated with it were frequently the subject of newspaper articles.

A more intimate acquaintanceship resulted while McCulloch was testing some of his outboards at the Salton Sea, and Holly Corporation began to peddle some of the nearby alkali flats and desert sand as recreational properties.

By the time McCulloch acquired his 13,000 acres of public land, he had also acquired the Holly Corporation to sell it, on what amounted to a commission basis. Later, the Holly Development portion of the Holly Corporation was purchased by McCulloch, but in the beginning, the firm simply acted as a real estate broker and worked on percentage.

In an interview, an informant who works for a company associated with the McCulloch Corporation said, "McCulloch Properties hired Holly for two reasons: a. They had massive expertise in large-scale sales projects. b. They had already gone through the throes of being investigated and chastised for some bad things they had done, and McCulloch hired them because they knew there was no way in the world they could do anything wrong, they couldn't afford to."

The latter reason seems somewhat specious. By the same reasoning, banks should only hire convicted embezzlers to handle money, an idea most bankers would deem a bit risky. If this was the actual reason, Robert McCulloch and C. V. Wood, Jr., the prime movers at Lake Havasu City, were naïve indeed.

It seems highly unlikely.

The same informant said, "M. Penn Phillips had a knack for staying within the law, but knowing just how far he could go."

One of the M. Penn Phillips disciples with the Holly Corporation was a sales manager by the name of Lorne B. Pratt. Pratt had established a good rapport with

McCulloch and other members of his staff, and by 1964 had done an excellent job of selling himself to the company. In commenting on the later purchase of Holly Development Company by McCulloch Properties, Laurence Laurie, head of the PR firm employed by McCulloch, said, "What we bought was Lorne Pratt."

Pratt's obvious approach was to show the McCulloch organization how they could avoid the pitfalls that Holly Corporation had stumbled on, yet come up with an irresistible sales formula. Needing a viable sales effort, Pratt's background, ideas, and sales training techniques fit smoothly into McCulloch's plans for Lake Havasu City.

Before exploring these sales techniques in action, it is necessary to take a look at the unusual municipal structure that was set up to govern Lake Havasu City.

In 1963, McCulloch technically sold some of the private land he had purchased at Lake Havasu to nine persons who promptly signed a petition requesting the establishment of an irrigation and drainage district at Lake Havasu. An irrigation and drainage district was described in the Arizona statutes as "a municipal corporation for all purposes."

An authoritative source connected with the McCulloch Corporation said, "The IDD [irrigation and drainage district] was one of the key things that made it possible without coming up with eight or ten times the front money you would normally need. Arizona's laws made it possible to have an organization which could authorize and sell bonds which could be used for water and streets."

Acting on the petition, the Mohave County board of supervisors set an election date for the district, and on September 20, 1963, six persons voted to affirm the district and elected Arnold and Carla Dutton to the first board of directors along with C. V. Wood, Jr. the top executive for the McCulloch project. In January 1964, these six voters held a bond election and approved a total of $7.14 million in bonds of which $1 million worth was sold for city improvements. This action committed *future* lot-buyers to the payment of the community's streets, water facilities and other public facilities. It also meant that through use of the IDD device, Lake Havasu City was essentially a company town owned lock, stock, and sagebrush by McCulloch Properties, Inc.

It has been alleged that four of the persons who voted in the establishment and the bond election for the district were not actual residents of the district, and as such were not entitled to vote. It was also alleged that five years after the election, the land which these four "residents" supposedly owned was deeded back to McCulloch Properties, and that it was set up solely for the purpose of establishing the irrigation and drainage district.

The current Mohave county attorney, Dave Babbitt, a cousin of the present Arizona attorney general, contends that the establishment of the irrigation and drainage district was misleading, if not an outright fraud. Babbitt says if you go through the papers on the initial filing for the IDD you will find the evidence to back up this contention. "You will find they refer to at least one section of farmland initially, and some more coming, and just as a sideline there would be a few thousand lots." Other than the sod farm near the landing strip, to grow grass for the golf courses, there was no agricultural land in the area at the time, and none contemplated. "Then as the first bond issue comes up all mention of agriculture starts to phase out," Babbitt explains. "That to me is wrong!" Babbitt states. "Fraudulent? I don't know. I am just saying it was basically wrong because it was misleading. The formation of the irrigation district was not to irrigate farmland—

that's what irrigation districts are set up to do—it was to develop and pay for the improvements and subdivision and furnished the front money for development."

Again, the end justified the means.

For a purpose, a goal, that McCulloch executives, state officials, and many within the Arizona business community thought worthwhile, deception, lies, bribery of various sorts, and the twisting, bending, and breaking of the law was permitted, if not condoned. Dazzled by the prospects of fame and fortune, they apparently gave little weight to the moral principles they espoused on Sunday.

A new city on the banks of the Colorado, a new frontier, growth in a barren desert, new jobs in new factories, a Palm Springs with water, free enterprise on the move, and of course that glorious feeling when someone you respect says, "Hey! you were really shrewd!"—these visions danced in their heads.

Who stopped to ask, "Is this right?" Certainly not the salesmen.

The sales techniques brought to the Lake Havasu project were several steps up the ladder of sophistication, and eliminated many of the crudities which were commonly present in many of the contemporary real estate scams of the period.

Many persons burned by land rip-offs in California and Florida were beginning to become cautious. The government and honest real estate men were telling the buying public that it was foolish to buy land sight unseen, especially land in remote desert areas or the swamps of Florida.

Developers were discovering that the old pie-in-the-sky schemes weren't paying off. A developer had to have something on the land to attract buyers. Golf courses, recreation centers, some homes already built, and paved streets in at least showplace portions of the development.

The sales plan developed by McCulloch Properties and Holly Development had a number of unusual features:

1. No property would be sold without the buyer having seen the property.

2. Air transportation to the site would be furnished free to prospective buyers.

3. Dual salesmen would be standard operating procedure, a generator and a closer.

4. Some promotional project would be undertaken which would generate nationwide publicity.

From a sales point of view, these features made a great deal of sense.

Psychologically, the requirement that a buyer must see the property would lend credibility to a business that was acquiring a very bad reputation. The air transportation to the site would create a feeling of obligation in the prospective buyer. The dual salesmen would make the buyer feel that he was dealing with a company rather than an individual who was only interested in his commission. Finally, the promotional project would give the company and the development enormous amounts of free advertising and by this national exposure foster the attitude that "it's so big, it's got to be good."

Those who have never been exposed to the sophisticated high-pressure pitch of a major land developer cannot appreciate the effectiveness of these carefully planned and well-calculated campaigns. Every avenue of buyer resistance has been thoroughly explored, and a battery of answers to fit every personality and situation has been inculcated in each and every salesman. It's awesome! Even supposedly sophisticated and level-headed people find themselves caught up in the psychologically perfected pitch.

They touch all bases, investment security for the future, a vacation retreat, a retirement community in the sun, healthful climate, no big-city smog or problems, snob appeal, and easy financing. They even throw in shills who have seen the light, and an auction atmosphere that's calculated to make you sign "now" before that good parcel of land is grabbed up by somebody else. For any person who has a cash reserve, even if it's small, it is almost impossible not to buy. They will even show you how to borrow money to come up with dollars needed to get your piece of the greatest real estate buy ever.

What makes it difficult to resist is the fact that there is always some grain of truth in their pitch. Lake Havasu, for example, is a lovely place, if you like sunshine, water, and the desert Southwest. All the positive aspects are stressed, and negative ones will soon be corrected. This is called salesmanship. But when promised corrections and plans are not forthcoming or even contemplated, and negative aspects are intentionally hidden, it is no longer salesmanship, it's just a con game.

In addition to its own experiences in California, Holly Development Company, the McCulloch sales organization, was able to observe the successful practices under way at Del Webb's Sun City, just west of Phoenix.

Construction at Sun City began in 1960, on 8,900 acres of farmland twelve miles northwest of Arizona's capital city, and though it was designed as a retirement community, the sales policies and techniques used at Sun City were in many cases applicable to the planned community concept at Lake Havasu.

When Sun City opened, the facilities were ready for use before the first lot was sold. In addition to model homes, the first recreation center was complete with swimming pool, shuffleboard courts, lawn bowling greens, arts and crafts studios, meeting and card rooms, and an auditorium. The first nine holes of the

North Golf Course were playable and the second nine were under construction.

A motor hotel with restaurant offered accommodations for visitors, and a shopping center provided new residents with most basic services.

During opening weekend, 272 homes were sold, and by the end of 1960, 1,301 units had been sold.

By the time Lake Havasu City was opened up for sale in 1964, Del Webb's Sun City had nearly 7,000 homes built.

The differences between the two developments were marked. One was established as a residential community for retirees, the other was ostensibly an industrial-recreational-retirement complex with an intermixed population. One was only a short distance from a major population center, while the other was more than one hundred miles from any large metropolitan area. Nevertheless, there were certain similarities.

Both were planned communities on a large scale, both were developed from raw land.

The real difference, however, was in such things as basic development policy and sales techniques.

While McCulloch Properties made an effort to have some facilities ready for their opening sales push, the Webb organization made sure these facilities were in place before they started to sell.

At Sun City, Webb limited residential sales to certain sections, and completely built up an entire neighborhood before opening up another section for sale. McCulloch, on the other hand, permitted purchases and "skip building" all over the 12,000 acres that were reserved as a residential area.

Partially due to its immediate success and partially due to company policy, Webb's organization used the soft-sell approach, which was extremely effective with the over-fifty buyer. McCulloch's sales crew, with some exceptions of course, utilized the sophisticated high-pressure tactics that it had acquired from the days with M. Penn Phillips.

Sun City salesmen didn't have to make promises with a dubious future; they could honestly say, "What you see is what you get." Over at Lake Havasu, it was a different story.

Prospective buyers would be contacted throughout the western half of the United States by salesmen known as generators. They would talk these potentials into taking a free plane trip on one of McCulloch's fleet of passenger aircraft to Lake Havasu, with no obligation, of course.

By the time a potential buyer stepped aboard a McCulloch plane, it was pretty well determined that he had the money and the inclination to buy. On board there was a variety of brochures and reading matter to hone the prospect's buying appetite. After circling to give the passengers a magnificent view of the Colorado River, the plane would land at the Site Six airstrip, where the potentials would be met by two large Greyhound buses and a bevy of salesmen known as closers.

The prospects were then whisked off to the Lake Havasu Hotel, where the real selling began.

Later they were taken on a guided tour of Lake Havasu City and shown the sites where things would be built in the future, and each prospective client had a closer at his side until the client either signed on a dotted line or left on the next flight out.

There is nothing essentially wrong with having a good sales program, if you sell what you have. Promises for the future are something else, especially when they are exaggerated, or when the risks and costs are hidden.

Another difference between Del Webb's Sun City and Lake Havasu City which should be emphasized is that Webb sold homes while McCulloch sold land. No one was permitted to purchase Sun City land for

137

speculation or "future building." Every sale included a house that fit the neighborhood. Lake Havasu City, however, was very loose in this regard, and land sales were the important emphasis, with homes, factories, etc. as a secondary factor.

While the current population of Lake Havasu City peaks out at about fourteen thousand persons, an estimated thirty thousand lots have been sold since 1964. This has created a patchwork of homes which gives a visitor to the area the impression that there has been insufficient planning and that the community lacks adequate facilities. Many people who have purchased land have simply been waiting for the price to go up. As a consequence their land remains vacant while these absentee landowners reside elsewhere.

In all fairness, it should be said that Robert McCulloch and C. V. Wood, Jr., did attempt to follow through on some of their promises, but, as it often is with businessmen who have made a heavy financial commitment, in their concern to recoup an investment they began to rely too heavily on sales and let the quality of their product slide.

McCulloch did build manufacturing facilities at Lake Havasu but by 1968, when it was stated in their 1964 press releases that a thousand-employee contingent would be operating, McCulloch was only producing about 10 per cent of its chain-saw parts in Havasu, and the number of employees was nowhere near the one thousand mark. In 1968, the power plant for the saw was still being produced in Los Angeles. This Los Angeles plant was the same one about which C. V. Wood, Jr., in his August 8, 1962, letter to the Department of the Interior had stated, "The Los Angeles plant is located directly across from the Los Angeles airport and the present land values ($300,000/acre) make it prohibitive to utilize the presently owned company land for manufacturing purposes. Therefore, site location studies were conducted to find an ideal location for the new home for the company."

In the same letter it was also stated, "The majority of the acreage surrounding the main factory (across from the Los Angeles International Airport), which was originally purchased for expansion purposes, has been sold."

In this same letter to the Department of the Interior it was implied that all of the Los Angeles plant production would be moved to the Site Six location. Such a move never occurred.

It seems that the initial enthusiasm to build extensive manufacturing facilities at Lake Havasu was tempered in a short while by the inability to get adequate personnel, and the discovery that it would be more advantageous to continue to do business in the Los Angeles area. As a consequence, the efforts to build industry along the Colorado became more cosmetic than actual. The sale of land then took over as the number-one priority.

Instead of developing Lake Havasu in digestible chunks, and permitting the quality of the development to sell itself, the McCulloch organization, anxious to convert its piles of sand into piles of money, took the ad man's approach.

Enter the London Bridge!

If there is one distinguishing feature of a McCulloch land development, it's gimmickry. Proper planned development in action is often slow and tedious, and its results and profits can take too much time for an active entrepreneur. Gimmickry, on the other hand, can produce immediate results, immediate traffic, and by a sheer volume of people immediate sales.

What could be more outrageous than buying the London Bridge and placing it in Arizona? They reasoned, and correctly, that the publicity would be enormous. Though it did little to improve Lake Havasu

139

City as a place in which to live and work, everyone in the nation and around the world would be conscious of Lake Havasu's existence. It might not improve the quality of the community, but it sure as hell would help sell the land.

The London Bridge that the McCulloch Oil Corporation purchased in 1968 for $2.46 million was the five-arch granite span completed in 1831 to replace the old wooden structure extant in Elizabethan times. The old wooden bridge, which also held a variety of shops, slowly collapsed over a period of time and gave rise to the tune, "London Bridge is falling down, falling down," etc. It is often confused by Americans with the "Tower Bridge," the Victorian span with the twin towers and a center section that could be raised and lowered to permit ships to pass under.

The McCulloch Corporation decided to buy it when the Corporation of London decided that a daily traffic load of 100,000 pedestrians and 10,000 vehicles was just too much for the "old girl" to carry, and a wider span was needed.

The structure was dismantled block by block, and each block was given a code number. The 22 million pounds of coded granite was then moved a quarter of the way around the earth, and the blocks were reassembled—all 10,276 of them—in precisely the same order in which they had been placed in England nearly a century and a half before.

The reassembling and the building of a new concrete-core structure, cost another $5 million. In total, nearly $7.5 million was spent for a bridge that wasn't needed. In fact, they had to dig a channel so that the waters of the Colorado could seep under the bridge and create a more "bridge-like" atmosphere.

True, the gimmick did bring nationwide attention to Lake Havasu City, but many still ask, "Did it help the community?"

Thousands of tourists and one-day gawkers drop in to see the London Bridge, but the community itself still doesn't have anywhere near the 28,000 population that the McCulloch releases said would be the case by 1976. Nor did McCulloch have a manufacturing facility employing 4,000 persons, as was estimated in their 1964 press release, for the year 1976.

Another grandiose advertising gimmick heralded another McCulloch development some twenty miles east of Phoenix. In a state with a severe water shortage, so they say, McCulloch Properties installed a lake in the middle of which spouts "the highest fountain in the world." The surrounding subdivisions are called "Fountain Hills."

Gimmicks are not confined to advertising, however. The sales practices at Lake Havasu are going to be probed by new Mohave County Attorney Dave Babbitt.

The probe was brought on by a charge that the original HUD report filed by McCulloch stated that streets within the city's boundaries were to be maintained by the district (IDD) at no cost to the buyers of property. Babbitt says he can verify this original HUD report, and said it is evidence of a glaring deception by the developer.

Evidence has also been presented to the Arizona attorney general's office in which HUD reports distributed in Arizona and HUD reports used in Minnesota were inconsistent with the Arizona Real Estate Department's property report on Lake Havasu City. The major inconsistencies present, according to an AG interoffice memo, were the fact that the various improvements to the property, such as roads, sewers, and water lines, were reflected as being installed at the developer's expense and not that of the land purchaser. Actually, all improvements are financed through the irrigation and drainage district, which then taxes property owners to retire the district's bonded indebtedness.

County Attorney Babbitt in an interview offered an example of this type of deception. "I talked to three people, all connected with county government, a supervisor, a county manager, and a finance director, all of whom are residents of Lake Havasu City. I asked each of them how they bought their property. I asked each of them if they had any knowledge or if at any time it was revealed to them that there were encumbrances against this land when they purchased it. Every one of them said no."

McCulloch representatives deny any sales hanky-panky, but admit that individual salesmen may have exaggerated a bit.

The allegations which may furnish evidentiary material for Babbitt's investigation surfaced at a recent meeting of the Mohave County board of supervisors after the board of directors of the Lake Havasu irrigation and drainage district asked the county to assume maintenance of the city's streets.

Babbitt, who attended the meeting, said, "By statutes, counties are obligated to maintain roads in unincorporated areas, and we may have no choice but to accept all of Lake Havasu City for maintenance."

A former county engineer reportedly said at the same meeting that he didn't think the county was liable, because McCulloch Properties did not meet county standards and failed to conform to its own HUD report specifications. As a result he contended the Lake Havasu City streets were not eligible for county maintenance.

It is clear that while the original objectives of McCulloch's top echelon and many of Arizona's important leaders were reasonably commendable, the methods used to achieve them left something to be desired. The big-time operators from California were just too clever to be good, and the Arizona leadership too greedy to be leaders.

Lake Havasu opened the door, and its lack of ethical and moral practices was the invitation that brought scam artists and criminals of all types to Arizona.

Chapter 8

THE POLITICIANS

The U. S. Attorney for Arizona, Mike Hawkins, stated in a recent television interview, "I don't think that land fraud could have grown and prospered in Arizona without an overall attitude in the agencies that regulate development companies that may have bordered on being illicit, and in some cases was in fact illicit. I don't believe it could have occurred without the tacit approval, cooperation, and even involvement of some public officials," Hawkins said.

Since the earliest territorial days, the Arizona politician has been associated with the "three C's" of economic power, Copper, Cattle, and Cotton. In 1966, however, a U. S. Supreme Court decision was implemented by which the "one man, one vote" principle caused legislative representation to shift from a rural bias to urban power. Now, many contend the Arizona politician is connected to the "three B's," Business, Banking, and Bonanno. The truth of this statement is speculation, but there is no doubt that with a diversification of the economy and an enormous population growth, Arizona politics has changed. While the powers of yesteryear strive to maintain their still considerable influence, Arizona economically and politically is beginning to ooze into the twentieth century.

The political philosophy espoused by most who run

for public office is self-described as conservatism. In Arizona, this means a privately oriented justice system, a right-to-work law, cheap labor (i.e., wetback aliens), the only state in the union without Medicaid, and a political attitude favorable to laissez-faire capitalism.

While its predominantly conservative press editorializes against the horrors of government spending, it hypocritically praises federally funded projects built within the state. And it is interesting to note that Arizona receives considerably more in federal funds than it pays to the federal government in taxes.

Its provincial conservatism can be demonstrated even in such minor examples as the fact that while there are several American Opinion bookstores in the Phoenix area there isn't one decent newsstand with out-of-town papers.

Currently, voter registration in the state slightly favors the Democratic party, but on election days the Republican party generally has a greater turnout of voters. However, any numerical advantage one way or the other has little bearing on the state's conservative nature, since a large body of Democrats are either Republicans who have registered as Democrats for local considerations, or conservative Democrats in the tradition of the Southern states.

Since over two thirds of the state's population was born elsewhere, Arizona has become a refuge for many who believe that here they can retreat to the simpler age of the frontier West—with air conditioning, of course. This belief, the sunshine, and the state's many acres of undeveloped land have caused an influx of retirees and others who can afford to indulge their fantasies of rugged individualism.

Prior to 1945, Republicans were a rare breed in the state, but the postwar boom brought a tremendous increase in persons who were willing to register under the GOP banner. By 1952, there was a sufficient number

146

for Barry Goldwater to defeat Ernest McFarland for the United States Senate, and conservatism in the state shifted from a time-worn Democratic party to a revitalized party of Arizona Republicans.

Barry Goldwater made his timely appearance on the conservative scene just as Senator Joseph McCarthy's career had peaked and began to falter.

To conservatives, Goldwater's outspoken, pithy brand of anti-liberalism and his Adam Smith economic philosophy were warmly received, especially in his home state of Arizona. This was particularly true in the laissez-faire atmosphere of the state's business community and the editorial offices of the Pulliam press, which controlled Phoenix's two major newspapers.

Not that the state's top Democrats weren't business-oriented, but they were tied too closely to Democratic administrations which had encouraged some regulation of business, and the local business tycoons much preferred a total absence of regulation.

Phoenix, the state's major city, was the Republican-conservative stronghold, and the political power of Phoenix more often than not controlled the state. Only in Tucson, where there is a Democratically oriented newspaper, the *Arizona Star*, were liberals like Stewart and Morris Udall able to gain and hold office over an extended period of time.

In a very real sense, Arizona did not begin to enter the twentieth century until World War II, when military establishments sprang up all over the state and brought in fresh blood from the outside world. A large number of servicemen found the sunshine and the open spaces attractive, and after the war they returned to Arizona as atom-age pioneers.

From 1940 to 1950, the population of Maricopa County (Phoenix area) climbed from approximately 150,000 to 331,000. It doubled again in the ten-year period 1950 to 1960, when the county's population figures showed 663,000. The rest of Arizona was nearly as spectacular.

Oddly enough, the fastest-growing age brackets in those two decades were in the "under fifteen" and "over sixty-five" categories. However, there were many married couples over fifty years of age that moved into the state, perhaps to escape the rigors of northern winters.

The milieu of politics was just right for the laissez-faire business community, and for the white collar criminals and organized-crime infiltrators who are often the camp followers of an irresponsible business community.

Currently significant politics in Arizona began about 1950. Prior to that the state was essentially run by conservatives and toadies who for purposes of acquiring federal funds for the state called themselves Democrats.

As the population explosion set in, new faces began to appear on the state's political scene. In 1950, for example, Barry Goldwater and Harry Rosenzweig were elected to the Phoenix city council as members of the new "charter government" slate, a non-partisan organization designed to rid the city of the blatant political corruption which had been entrenched in Phoenix for years. Pay-offs to council members to protect prostitution and gambling, and for various other favors, had prior to this time been carried on in the best traditions of Boss Tweed or James Michael Curley. It was as common as tipping a waiter. The "charter government" group was formed to combat this situation and to formulate a new city charter which could clean up the mess.

Backed by the Pulliam press and a business community looking for a "clean collar," the charter government group made rapid strides in its early days to do

148

the job for which it was intended. They threw the rascals out.

Harry Rosenzweig, commenting on that time, said, "Prior to our coming in, there had been what had seemed about thirty-five city managers in about thirty years, and each of these city managers had been picked not for their talent but because they were manageable. So we brought in Ray Wilson from Kansas City, an assistant to that city's manager, Cookingham, who had been very successful in organizing Kansas City after the Pendergast group. Ray turned out to be an excellent organizer," Rosenzweig declared. "He brought a few people with him who were professionals, and that was the beginning of a professional administration operated by professionals."

What this meant in reality was a new rider in the saddle. The old political hacks were out and personable members of the rapidly expanding business community were in.

From this political beginning, Barry Goldwater's career rose rapidly.

Well-known from his connection with the Goldwater department store chain and his activities in a wide variety of community affairs, Barry also began to take an interest in state politics, and became involved with the gubernatorial campaign of radio station executive Howard Pyle.

In an odd twist of fate, the political careers of Goldwater and Pyle were turned around almost at their beginnings. Ex-governor Howard Pyle explains, "Originally, he [Goldwater] was going to run for governor in '52, and I was going to run for the Senate, because I didn't have a family business here like the Goldwaters, who had a big store here. History didn't quite follow what was originally discussed," Pyle said with amusement, "but I think it was better the way it ended."

The turnabout came when Pyle was drafted in 1950 >

as the Republican candidate for governor by the state's Young Republicans group, and Barry Goldwater became his unofficial campaign manager.

Pyle relates, "He did in effect travel with me, and we were more or less just a couple of guys out there shooting for a mark. But I think we always thought of him as being the campaign manager."

In what has been regarded as the revitalization of the Republican party in Arizona, Howard Pyle eked out a narrow victory over Democrat Anna Frohmiller, the former state auditor.

With Pyle installed as governor of Arizona, Goldwater decided while still a city council member to go up against Ernest McFarland, who was at the time the majority leader in the United States Senate. McFarland had spent two terms in the Senate after defeating Henry Fountain Ashurst in 1940. As the majority leader, he was a powerful man and to many political observers he appeared unbeatable. However, the Korean war had left a bad taste in Arizona, and President Truman's firing of General MacArthur did nothing to aid the state's Democrats.

Stephen Shadegg, Goldwater's campaign director, remembers, "The time was ripe, Ike was running, and we were in an unpopular war. Then, McFarland made some unfortunate statements about it [the war]."

Shadegg details the McFarland blunder. "What happened was McFarland went down to Casa Grande, and he was discussing Korea. In the discussion he said, 'It's a cheap war, anyway,' and he meant that it *was* a cheap war, that it wasn't costing much money and we weren't losing many men."

Shadegg chuckled a bit, then continued, "We picked that up! We got a tape of his statement, and *we* said, 'When any American is dying it's not cheap, and no parent would consider it cheap.' Mac just ran a bad campaign, and we beat him!" Shadegg concluded.

Barry Goldwater was elected to the U. S. Senate in 1952 by a margin of a little over seven thousand votes.

It is interesting to note that Stephen Shadegg had been the campaign manager for venerable Democratic Senator Carl Hayden just two years previously in 1950.

Shadegg in an interview explained his position: "I was always an anti-Roosevelt, anti-Truman, anti-New Deal Democrat, but my connection with Hayden was a personal friendship, and I felt that he was a fine guy and the man running against him [in 1950] was not qualified. They wanted me to run the McFarland campaign in 1952, and I refused to do that," Shadegg declared.

It was also in 1952 that a young attorney from Mesa, Arizona, ran on the Republican ticket for Congress. His name was John J. Rhodes, and he too won his seat as U.S. representative from Arizona District #1. He's still there as Republican minority leader in the House of Representatives.

If there is anyplace in the United States that clearly demonstrates the foolishness of political party labels it is Arizona. While it appeared on the surface that Republicans were getting the upper hand over Democrats in the state in 1952, it was nothing more than new faces replacing the old as Arizona conservatives. Politically the real divisions in the state are: establishment right wing, far right wing, and liberals.

Since large-scale manufacturing still has not entered Arizona, and labor unions are a joke, the liberal element is small with very little influence. The one demonstratable exception in recent years was the 1964 election of Sam Goddard as governor. Considered by most as liberal, Goddard's image was made palatable by the endorsement of the establishment right-wing Pulliam press (the *Arizona Republic* and *Gazette*), and he was elected. But he was not re-elected, and remains the exception.

While conservatives are generally known as staunch law-and-order supporters, their support in Arizona is confined basically to street crime, drug abuse, or sex-related offenses. White collar or organized crime doesn't seem to generate the same fervor, perhaps because it may seem to reflect somehow on so-called free-enterprise practices. This can be seen in the state's feeble laws and the weak enforcement of existing laws regarding business-related crimes.

According to Adam Smith's *The Wealth of Nations*, the production and exchange of goods, and a consequent rise in the general standard of living, can be attained only through the efficient operations of private industrial and commercial entrepreneurs, acting with a minimum of regulation and control by governments. The advocacy of this theory in Arizona undoubtedly contributed toward an atmosphere fertile for the philosophies of Barry Goldwater, the John Birch Society, and the minions of the Mafia.

The lack of regulation and control over white collar and organized crime in Arizona and the subsequent boldness in criminal practices offer justification for the statement that reporter Don Bolles died from the conscience of a conservative.

Nowhere is the cause of private vested interest more pragmatically expressed than in the Arizona Legislature.

In Arizona, the legislature is a bicameral body consisting of thirty members of the State Senate and sixty members of the House of Representatives, and they receive as compensations for their efforts a glorious salary of $6,000 per annum, and a per diem allotment while in session. As a result, Arizona legislators must either be financially well off, have a job or income that requires little of their time, or be willing to accept extra compensation from those willing to pay for legislative favors. There is no way a person can feed, clothe, and house a family on $6,000 per year in Arizona. In addition, they must come up with an average of about $3,000 for campaign expenses every time they run, and in the House there is a re-election every two years.

Ross R. Rice, writing in the book *Politics in the American West*, says of the Arizona Legislature, "Interest groups realize their objectives in the Arizona Legislature through two principal avenues. First, some groups have built-in access through overlapping memberships in the Legislature, and second, some engage in lobbying. Two economic interests in particular have profited from built-in access, the mining corporations and the cattle ranchers. For years certain legislators, especially senators, admitted wearing *copper collars.*"

This is still true to a certain extent, but in recent years powerful lobbies have had the greater impact. The banks and public utilities such as the Arizona Public Service Company and the Salt River Project have acquired enormous influence through lobbying. Recently, the amalgam of business interests in the state has consolidated its efforts through the lobbying presence of the Arizona Chamber of Commerce. The Arizona Taxpayers' Association, reportedly supported by banks and utilities, and the business-oriented Arizona Academy are having an increasingly important effect on legislation.

Ex-governor Sam Goddard commented in an interview on the problems he had with the Legislature and the Arizona establishment during his term in office. In response to the question, "What was your greatest problem or pressure while in office?" he replied, "If you want to know what we *really* had to fight, and it got to me, it's basically what the IRE (Investigative Reporters and Editors) was trying to put their finger on, and the reason they were so scared of it, the 'good old boy' league, where a 'good old boy' got a piece of this, and a 'good old boy' got a piece of that."

Goddard continued, "The first thing I did to mess that up was to change the way the Legislature appropriated money. Originally, the big departments used to lobby their own appropriations through, and the bigger departments [state] with more jobs were able to make a pretty good thing for themselves. The little departments that didn't have much were never able to do very well. But when we got the 'governor's budget' through that short-circuited the business of hanky-panky."

He also pointed out some of the problems attending the State Highway Department. "It was a tradition that when your man from your county got on the Highway Commission, he pillaged for his county for the length of his term. You would see a road that would be built for a ways, then all of a sudden it would stop. That was when your highway commissioner got off the commission," he said.

At one time, the sale of state jobs was quite an acceptable practice, Goddard charged. He said that in 1962, a group of "good old boys" who were backing his opponent had set up an organization for this purpose. "They set up in all earnestness, and publicly, something that I'll never be able to understand as long as I live, called the 'Ten-Ten' club. If you gave them ten bucks [per month] they would give you a guarantee of a job. Give them one hundred bucks and they would give you a better job. If you gave them a thousand bucks you'd be given your choice of jobs," Goddard related. "They did this publicly," he said, "and I was able to meet with them at one time in which they openly admitted, 'Why, sure, that's the way politics is done, and we'll guarantee you a state job.' It's hard to believe," Goddard continued, "but this was only 1962."

This group, according to Goddard, was composed of many old-time ranchers, as well as those with mining and agricultural interests who had an extraordinary influence on the state Legislature.

Reciting another legislative practice he encountered upon taking office as governor, Goddard said, "I found that the state insurance was contracted out, almost entirely, to members of the state Legislature. I found out that the president of the state Senate [Clarence Carpenter] had one of the biggest wads of insurance of anybody. Carp's insurance agency ran on that state stuff!

"It was in the governor's purview," he continued, "so I pulled all of that money out, and set up a system where anybody in the state who ran an insurance company could make an open bid on the thing, and it could be distributed out without any reference to politics.

"They never forgave me for that," Goddard concluded. "Believe me!"

Many of the shenanigans of the 1960s are said to have been wiped out through public pressure. They were just too blatantly corrupt for even a conservative populace to stomach.

Since the death of Don Bolles, some anti-crime legislation has wiggled its way through the Legislature. However, the current edition (1977 Legislature) is still responsive to the blandishments of powerful private interests.

The defeat of House Bill 2018 in the Arizona Senate this year is an example of how a selfish, irresponsible business community can control the Legislature, even on a measure that was designed as a body blow to white collar crime.

Last year, after the death of Don Bolles, when everyone was screaming to "clean up the state" and rip apart organized crime in memory of the courageous reporter, an amendment was slipped through the Legislature. This supposed clarification measure eliminated a

155

previous state requirement that Arizona corporations must file annual financial statements. It also made the destruction of corporate records a misdemeanor, like smoking in an elevator. At the very moment that the state's leadership, including the members of the Legislature, were beating their breasts over Bolles' brutal murder, this investigative tool, "corporate financial statements," was being relegated to the garbage can, and the destruction of records, which had been a felony, was turned to a slap on the wrist.

Arizona Republic investigative reporter Al Sitter expressed his dismay over this action in a penetrating by-line article. Sitter's story stunned a few people, and in its spotlight the Arizona Legislature squirmed.

House Majority Leader Burton Barr, a Republican, said, "I'd like to have had a net to get that back. That got through on a corporation act, and when they called me, and told me that this thing had gotten through, I was shocked, I frankly didn't know it had gone through. We're going to correct it, it shouldn't have gotten through the first time."

This year, Representative Jim Skelly, a Republican from Scottsdale, proposed a bill (HB-2018) which would require the filing of financial returns and would reinstitute the destruction or altering of corporate records as a felony. This bill sailed through the House without a single vote against it (57 to 0).

It was then brought up in the Arizona Senate, where it was promptly killed.

How and why did it happen?

Republic columnist Bernie Wynn, in commenting on the Senate defeat of the measure, said, "The Republican leadership in the Arizona Senate must be suffering from a severe myopia or it deliberately is trying to reassure the public the GOP is the party of fat cats."

By a vote of 17 to 12, all Republicans save one, Senator Robert B. Usdane of Scottsdale, and four conservative Democrats voted down this Republican-sponsored house bill.

The Senate had a similar bill which was killed in committee; then during the first week of April 1977 they took up the House version, which had passed that body without a single dissenting vote. Some investigation revealed that between the time the bill left the House of Representatives and the time it reached the floor of the state Senate a powerful campaign to kill the measure was instituted by the businessmen's lobby, the Arizona Chamber of Commerce.

Robert Robb, lobbyist for the Arizona Chamber of Commerce, while denying that he lobbied the Senate to vote down the bill, said, "What we did was try to urge upon every member of the Legislature the principle that a corporation has certain rights to privacy." This lobbying and the efforts of certain Republican senators changed what had been a "motherhood and apple pie" attitude toward the measure in the House to one of deep concern in the Senate.

While the Senate was considering its similar bill in the finance committee, Senator Ray Rottas of Phoenix introduced an amendment which had the blessing of the Arizona Chamber of Commerce. The "Rottas amendment" would limit access to law enforcement officials, and prevent the news media and the public from checking to see if corporations were as they represented themselves.

Rottas explained his reasons for the amendment: "This time around we figured as representatives of the business community we would do what we could to retain the concept of some privacy to corporate shareholders."

Senate Minority Leader Leo Corbet, Republican, was reported as saying that he opposed the measure because, "It won't get the bad guys and it will penalize the good guys. The crooks aren't going to put down anything they don't want you to see," he said.

When the house bill reached the Senate floor, an attempt to add the Rottas amendment was defeated after lengthy debate during which Senator Corbet argued the Rottas proposal would "allow us to catch the crooks. But what Mom and Pop are doing at their store, how much money they make, is no one's business."

After this watering-down amendment was actually defeated on a straight party-line vote, the ensuing vote on the bill itself saw four Democrats, Senators Polly Getzwiller of Casa Grande, Tom Moore of Tucson, Bill Swink of San Manuel, and Senate president Ed Sawyer of Safford, suddenly switch over to the Republican side and reject the measure 17 to 12. One of the senators who had fought for the measure, Senator Sue Dye of Phoenix, said, "For whatever reasons, it was a miserable performance on the part of the Senate."

In Arizona, it seemed to prove once again that whatever business wants business gets.

When it was mentioned to a top federal law enforcement official that the Arizona Chamber of Commerce had lobbied against House Bill 2018 in the Senate, he replied, "I can't think of a better reason to pass it."

The effect of the state's powerful private lobbies on regulatory legislation is prodigious, yet little has been done by the state's news media to inform the public on who these lobbyists are, and who they represent. There is also little publicity given to the voters of individual legislators, particularly in committee hearings.

It is often said by men who run for public office that the public expects too much from its political leaders, and perhaps this is true at times. While it is possible for anyone to make a mistake, or to be misinformed, it is also true that politicians are essentially representatives of their general constituency, and their actions are supposed to reflect the will of all their electorate.

In Arizona, public input to elected representatives is meager indeed, and often all a legislator will hear on a subject are the carefully chosen words of a professional lobbyist. Yet members of the news media who cover the Legislature often ask whether a lack of public interest is sufficient reason for a lack of public concern by its elected leaders.

Just as the state's politicians are hyper-responsive to vested business interests, they are also sensitive to water.

Since the 1920s, Arizona's establishment has been trying to get the U.S. government to bring more water to central Arizona. Led by Senator Carl Hayden, every major politician to emerge in the state has been a spokesman for the Central Arizona Project, the multi-billion-dollar water-delivery system that President Jimmy Carter tried to cut from the national budget.

It's a sacred cow to the Arizona establishment.

As a spokesman for the CAP, the Arizona politician is also a spokesman for the central Arizona farming interests, the state's largest public utilities, the banks, the insurance companies, and the land owners and developers who have invested in this part of the state. Agriculture uses 90 per cent of the state's water, and the mining industry in southern Arizona is a large user of the remaining 10 per cent.

Over the years the proponents of the CAP have attempted to peddle the fiction that the major population centers would soon dry up and blow away if the Central Arizona Project was not built. This is nonsense! What has happened is that farmers have overdeveloped lands in sections of the state that have an insufficient water supply. As a consequence, there has been an overdraft of groundwater, the water table has dropped, and expenses to pump the water deep in the ground

159

have soared. Hydrologists agree that there is plenty of water to serve the needs of the urban centers for many years to come, but the enormous requirements of agriculture in central Arizona cannot be met.

Since the financial and political power of the state is centered in central Arizona, the powers-that-be would much rather saddle the federal government and the taxpayers of the state with the Central Arizona Project that develop new cities and new lands in the western part of the state near the Colorado River. Oddly enough, even the proponents of the CAP agree that it will not solve the problem. What it will do, however, is make it possible for current farming interests to suck the last full measure from the land before they move on, and it will make water available to large hunks of desert land which speculators have bought in anticipation of further urban growth. Again, what business wants business gets, even if it comes out of the public pocket.

Yet, despite the obvious subservience to the state's business establishment, few of the nation's major manufacturing firms are contemplating a move to Arizona.

Ex-governor Sam Goddard gives an explanation of this phenomenon: "When an industry tries to move into a state they usually do a rather substantial study of what goes on in a state, and one of the things they look at is what do the local people do about their problems, especially crime and the building of public facilities. We have not been overrun by people trying to move into Arizona to conduct large industrial enterprises. We've had a few headquarters operations and Motorola," Goddard stated.

He blamed the apathetic approach in the state to problems of crime and a lack of social consciousness as the reasons for Arizona's inability to attract these industries.

"Now, we're going to have to do a very 'hard sell' in

160

order to reverse the idea that everybody is out here waiting with some kind of a scalpel to fleece the people and sell them rattlesnake land."

What this all suggests is that the politicians in Arizona, generally speaking, have ignored the real needs of the state, and have perpetuated an ambience which has given rise to crime and unethical business practices. Rather than leading the way and telling lawyers and businessmen to "clean up their act," they have prostituted their public trust for private gain.

Chapter 9

THE BUSINESSMEN '

Dr. Brent Brown, executive director of the Arizona governor's Office of Economic Planning and Development, who has the job of attracting business to the state, says that the business climate in Arizona is good despite the concern being voiced over the state's crime problems.

"Some people from other sections of the country now ask us whether Arizona is run by the Mafia," Brown suggested in a newspaper interview [*Phoenix Gazette*]. "But we tell those considering moving their business here that steps are being taken to correct problems. We tell them government here doesn't overspend and is interested in business," Brown said.

Brown and the various chambers of commerce are the paid stimulators of that economic cancer called uncontrolled growth. While these salesmen for the state profess an interest in controlled and directed growth, they actually grab what they can in the belief that growth is good, regardless.

"Let's face it!" they say. "Arizona is one of the fastest-growing states in the nation, and we should let the marketplace determine what is going to succeed or fail in the state."

The restrictions here are few, and this they believe is

one of the best pitches available to attract the out-of-stater who wants to get into the Arizona swim.

These salesmen are aided and abetted by the migratory shift of the nation's population.

The U. S. Bureau of the Census report released November 24, 1976, said that America's population is flowing south and west in increasing numbers. This could, the bureau says, cause dramatic shifts in political power. Florida and Arizona are rated the fastest-growing states. Arizona's population grew 25 per cent from 1970 to 1975, while Florida had a net growth of 1.6 million, a number roughly equal to the population of the entire state of Nebraska. Climate, lower taxes, and cheaper land were considered among the major factors contributing to the emergence of the sun belt states as growth centers for the nation.

Bureau of the Census spokesman David Word said, "Another factor is the large number of elderly persons choosing to move to Florida and Arizona for their retirements."

This is *not* natural growth, however.

The Bureau study broke down its population figures into two categories: natural growth, caused by the difference between births and deaths, and growth caused by migration from one state to another. Natural growth was down in all states, because of declining birth rates, according to the Bureau of the Census.

Ken Ross, chief economist at the First National Bank of Arizona, says, "This has been a growth area since the post-World War II days. We were growing real fast, and whether by design or oversight just didn't do some of the planning that should have been done. Some of our cities have an urban sprawl," Ross continued. "Phoenix is a good example of an 'uncontrolled growth,' but they're beginning to recognize that now."

This belief may be wishful thinking or an unwarranted assumption.

For example, Peter D. Herder, national representative for Arizona in the National Association of Home Builders, writing in the December 23, 1976, edition of the *Arizona Real Estate Reviews and News*, said, "Are we really serving the needs of the public health, safety, and general welfare with the multitude of regulations and ordinances? When our housing needs are greater today than ever before, can it legitimately be stated that our growth rate and development has been too great in the past, and, therefore, must be limited in the future? What rational justification can be provided by local government when declaring a moratorium on development for the purpose of putting its own house in order? Where will needed housing be constructed if every community did the same?"

This comment is interesting in light of the fact that the bulk of Arizona's residential building is not for the low-income families who need housing, but for those Arizonans and out-of-staters who can afford it.

In response to a question on whether the growth syndrome has contributed to the movement of organized-crime money into Arizona, bank economist Ken Ross said, "I don't know, but just as a casual observer, that kind of money would tend to be attracted to a growth area such as this. Again, primarily because we're so busy growing we don't pay attention to that money coming in."

Just who and what are the major controlling powers in the Arizona business establishment? The answer was succinctly given by state House Majority Leader Burton Barr, who is also a businessman.

"We're provincial. We've grown in numbers, but the power structure of the community is pretty much the same as when I got here twenty-five years ago. In other words, the major interests [of that time] are still the power structure, and the lawyers who represent the Bar Association in the main represent those major interests," he said. "I think they [the power structure] have great influence with the paper [*Arizona Republic* and *Gazette*] and in any area they want to move. The Phoenix Forty to a great extent represents a lot of that power structure," Barr elaborated.

The Phoenix Forty is described as a group of the city's most influential business and community leaders, and Phoenix is the most influential city in the state. The organization is composed of top executives in banking, the legal profession, real estate, manufacturing, advertising, the news media, the utilities, and other organizations who are prominent in the Arizona business establishment. Its primary function is to lobby and apply public and private pressure on government for causes it deems worthwhile and important. In a sense it is the chamber of commerce for the chambers of commerce in Arizona, the inner council for the business establishment of the state.

Some have called it the conscience of the commercial community, the round table of virtuous purpose, or the moral activists of legitimate business.

Others feel differently.

One of the top law-enforcement officials in the state commented recently, "Somebody called me up the other day and asked me if I wanted to speak before the Phoenix Forty on what has caused the public malaise or attitude that has fostered the crime problem. I told them, 'I decline the invitation, and if you want to know what it is, what entity or institution created such an attitude, I suggest that you call a meeting [of the Phoenix Forty] and give everybody there at the meeting a mirror.' "

There are others in the state who feel the same way.

Whether it is justified or simply an obvious result of frustration, there is a feeling abroad in the land that the Phoenix Forty more closely approximates a Cosa

Nostra in Arizona than the suspicioned activities of Joe Bonanno or Peter Licavoli.

Periodically, the Phoenix Forty will issue public statements condemning or condoning certain individuals or actions, but recently it has been rather quiescent. James Simmons, president of the United Bank, and head of the Phoenix Forty's Crime Task Force, says, "The Phoenix Forty is still active and has its Crime Task Force active still. It continues to have meetings with people involved in the law-enforcement area. But the Phoenix Forty is also involved in other areas. The reason you don't see a lot of publicity on it," Simmons continued, "is that it is not the intention of our group to be highly visible, except when we feel it is necessary to do so."

He explained the structure of the Phoenix Forty: "It's not a day-to-day activity; it's not even formally organized. It's just a group of people who meet at least once a month, and with a number of operating committees who are dedicated to certain projects, one of which is crime."

Simmons viewed the role of the Phoenix Forty as the business-community support for those whose jobs were to attack crime.

In response to a question as to what the Phoenix Forty was doing to clean up white collar crime, James Simmons replied, "The Phoenix Forty is not operational in that field to the extent that we would seek out or try to do the job of any governmental agency. I guess what our main function is, or at least what we felt we could do effectively, was to determine if the various law-enforcement facets were doing the job, and of course that would include getting out the bad apples in business as well as getting out the bad apples who might be robbing a Circle K [convenience market]. We're not a vigilante group, and don't pretend to be. What we're trying to do is see that good people are in the offices [law enforcement], and see that they have the money and means to do the job," Simmons said.

To some people in the state, this simply means that the Phoenix Forty's contribution to the fight against crime is to encourage the state, city, and county to spend some more public funds to solve the problem when in fact they could do a great deal more by a concerted effort to upgrade the moral and ethical standards of Arizona businessmen.

For example, the Phoenix Chamber of Commerce in a published letter to the editor stated, "The image and reputation of Arizona is being badly tarnished nationally by overzealousness in reporting *possible* wrongdoing by members of the business community in general and the land-development community in particular.

"The treatment that Lake Havasu City received recently from the press is a case in point," it continued.

The letter concluded by saying, "It does not seem too much to ask that the press refrain from emotional nitpicking over relatively *inconsequential* complaints."

It was signed by the entire executive committee of the Phoenix Metropolitan Chamber of Commerce.

"If the concern expressed by law-enforcement officials and others over the corruption of public officials, the giveaway of public lands, the rip-off practices of land salesmen, and other seamy acts involved in the Havasu affair is inconsequential, perhaps the Phoenix Forty could organize a Sunday school class teaching business ethics and morality to the Phoenix Chamber of Commerce," was a published response of one Phoenician.

Among the most powerful business organizations in the state are such banks as the Valley National Bank, the First National Bank of Arizona, United Bank, Great Western Bank, the Continental Bank, and the Thunderbird Bank, with Valley and First National the biggest and most influential.

The top utilities are Arizona Public Service, Salt River Project, and Tucson Gas and Electric.

In real estate, the power and the money reside in the state's title insurance and trust companies. Such firms as Trans-America Title, Minnesota Title, American Title, Arizona Title, Chicago Title, Commonwealth Land Title, St. Paul Title, Pioneer National, Lawyers Title, Stewart Title, and U. S. Life Title Company of Arizona are the real beneficiaries of land transactions in the state.

Since the real estate scams have given Arizona a good portion of its bad reputation, the role of the title company bears some scrutiny.

The current state land commissioner of the state of Arizona is Andrew L. Bettwy, and he presents a rather clear picture of the protagonists in an Arizona real estate transaction.

Between the seller and the buyer in any transaction you generally have a broker and a title company, both of whom exist and make their money by a transaction taking place. Since the seller, the broker, and the title company are anxious for the deal to go through, the buyer is at their mercy unless he hires a lawyer to look after his interests.

In 1962, the constitution of the state of Arizona was amended to permit real estate brokers to handle the legal paper work in real estate transactions.

Commissioner Bettwy contends this was a mistake. "In my opinion, I think you could trace most of the problems in this state from the date of that constitutional amendment. What that did generally," Bettwy continued, "was take the lawyers out of the real estate field.

"In the early sixties, it was a big deal! The title companies were mad because the Bar Association brought suit against them for practicing the law, and there was no question that they were. But they got their guns together, the in-house attorneys for the title companies, and the amendment was put through," Bettwy said.

Bettwy believes the title companies have not properly informed the buyers of Arizona real estate as to the specifics of what the buyer is actually buying.

"You'll see these big signs that say 'Snake Acres' or whatever it is, and it'll also say 'Title guaranteed by—' " Bettwy commented.

"Every one of these land deals has a beautiful title policy," the land commissioner continued, "and I'm sure there are thousands of them running around that on the face of them it showed that the people didn't get anything. Not a damn thing! Then the title company says, 'Hell, we told you in there that you weren't getting anything!' and the buyer says, 'You mean to tell me that I'm supposed to read four pages of that kind of print that says what I wasn't supposed to get, and then this other stuff that's in larger print but I don't even know the sequence of it?' Then the title company says, 'Well, that's all that's our function, so we sold you the policy,' " Bettwy said.

To oversimplify, a title company is basically a business that searches out the legal ownership of property, and in most cases guarantees or ensures the correctness of the information it finds. Of course, title companies get involved in many complex ways in the sale of land and real property, as evidenced by the huge skyscrapers that house their offices in Phoenix and elsewhere. They are real money-makers.

One may stupidly ask, "Are title companies really necessary?"

Land Commissioner Bettwy in response to such a question pointed out, "In the nation of Mexico, you can go to any public property registry in that country, and for ten pesos you can get a statement that tells you the status of that land, and the statement is legal and enforceable."

When asked if there was anything similar in the United States, he replied, "A couple of states have what they call the Torrens title system; it's the Torrens system of recording. You go to your state government and get your certificate right there.

"All the information the title companies get, they get for the recorder's office. All this state would have to do is record by legal description instead of recording by name," he said.

Bettwy expressed that hopeless feeling often encountered by concerned officials: "I used to advocate that Torrens system. I ran for the Legislature one time, and tried to explain it, but, hell! No one paid any attention."

Bettwy also pointed out that under current state law, the seller and the broker are not liable for fraudulent practices and that the only recourse available to a buyer is the extent of the coverage he has in the title insurance policy that he purchased at the time of the sale.

Responding to the question, "What is the most important thing that could be done to prevent land fraud?" Bettwy replied, "It's very simple. I would take *every* party to the transaction, and I would make them jointly and separately liable, and I would get the lawyers back into the field, not because I'm a lawyer. But I would take the title company, the broker, and the seller, and if they had a lawyer on that side, and those people would be responsible if fraud was perpetrated. I can't see why anybody in that group should be excused, because all they would have to do is to let the buyer know what he is getting."

Most buyers, Bettwy contends, do not have the sophistication fully and accurately to interpret these title company insurance policies.

To point up this contention, Albert J. Sitter, one of the stalwarts in Arizona's tiny band of investigative reporters, revealed that a former Army captain bought a parcel of land in response to an ad in *Stars and Stripes*, the U. S. Armed Forces' overseas newspaper, only to find out later that there was no legal access to the property.

The land in question, near U.S. 40 about thirty miles northeast of Holbrook, is adjacent to the Petrified Forest National Monument, and was purchased four years ago by Clyde O. Peterson from the Cholla Land and Cattle Company of Phoenix. It's part of the 7,000-acre Stonewood Ranch subdivision acquired by Cholla through a trust agreement administered by Minnesota Title and Trust.

Peterson said in a follow-up interview, "At the time I bought it [four years ago] everything was fine [regarding access], it was going to go right down my property line, and all that nonsense. They lied!" he said.

Peterson, who is also a retired contractor, contended that the Cholla Company officials and their lawyer later promised that the access problem would be solved by the time he arrived in Arizona in July of 1975, but nothing ever happened.

Peterson said he had plans to build a ninety-unit motel, lodge, and restaurant on the property, but the lack of access prevented it.

Peterson, who said he paid about $18,000 for his purchase, had made regular monthly payments to Minnesota Title for the property. It was his belief, he alleged, that the title company knew the property had no access from the very outset because it is surrounded by federal and railroad-owned land.

Apparently, businessmen who peddle land without access are not new in Arizona. The planning director for Coconino County, Hank Hoag, has warned buyers of land in northern Arizona. Hoag reportedly said some 650 to 1,000 acres of land are being sold in Coconino

172

County each month without state supervision. He said that while the procedure used is legal, it presents some problems to buyers.

In some cases, he said, the land has no roads, with instances in which the nearest road is twenty miles away. In other cases, there is no legal access to the land.

The planning director said the land sellers get around subdivision regulations because the original parcels were over 36 acres in size and exempt from state law. According to Hoag, several efforts have been made to close the loophole in the Legislature but to no avail.

As for the title companies, Don Bolles, writing in an *Arizona Republic* article in 1969, said, "Most home buyers don't realize how they are affected by title insurance and escrow agents. The real estate salesman quotes a price of a home to them, including some mumbo-jumbo about added fees and costs. After a couple of weeks, the deed and supply of monthly mortgage-payment cards show up. Sure enough, they did throw in added costs.

"The transaction during that time has usually been in the hands of an escrow agent, most often a title company. An escrow agent is a middleman between buyer and seller—sort of an impartial umpire who is supposed to make sure both get the money and papers to which each is entitled."

Bolles quoted a client who was dissatisfied with Transamerica, the largest title company in Arizona. The client, Harvey Gibbs, who had filed suit against the firm, said, "It's a nice closed deal, you pay the title insurance companies good money to protect you from unknown claims against the land you buy. And if they mess up, your only recourse is to sue. The title company may know it will lose the case, but they have the

173

money and lawyers to outwait you. Sooner or later, most of the little guys cave in.

"One thing I've discovered: It's hard to get a decent lawyer to take your case. That's because the title companies farm out their cases to most of the reputable law firms, and those firms have to turn down any suits against the companies because of conflict of interest."

Title insurance companies are not the only firms to come under fire; the insurance industry in general has caused some retching.

State Insurance Commissioner Jack Trimble is quoted as saying that Arizona's insurance laws are "a laughingstock" which make it easy for fraudulent companies to operate in the state. He said that a segment of Arizona's insurance industry is presenting nearly as bad a national image for Arizona as the land fraud problems.

There are approximately fourteen hundred insurance companies in the state. Twenty-two per cent of all the insurance firms in the nation are headquartered in Arizona. Why? All that's necessary to start one in Arizona is $25,000 front money and $1,200 in surplus cash, that's why!

Insurance Commissioner Trimble said that there are literally hundreds of insurance companies who have their headquarters in Arizona, but all their agencies are out-of-state, which makes any state regulation difficult. Trimble said the weak laws have produced a number of insurance scams and rip-offs. Among them was the channeling of $2 million to the Swiss bank account of one firm's director, the non-payment of claims, and involvement with real estate frauds.

"It is amazing how you see some names come up again and again, with some of these guys seemingly building assets out of air," he is quoted as saying.

"The biggest area of insurance fraud," Trimble said, "is in reinsurance." This is the practice where firms ostensibly help each other to cover large policies, and in Arizona some of these firms financially overextend themselves and sell more insurance than they can cover.

Trimble said, however, that the fraudulent companies were a very small percentage of the total number incorporated in the state.

The same can be said for most businesses in Arizona; the owners would prefer to operate ethically. There is, however, tremendous pressure from monopolies, greedy individuals, and unethical quick-money specialists which can force marginal business operations to cut corners as a matter of survival. Some prominent Arizonans have suggested that a lack of ethics is more evident in the larger, controlling powers of the state's business community, where arrogance born of dominating influence places ethical considerations on the back burner.

A Phoenix-area newspaper editor said, "You have [in Arizona] a power structure of three or four big law firms, the banks, a few very large powerful industries, and the Pulliam people. They are the Paradise Valley and Phoenix Country Club people and they run the town. They run it to make money and they don't give a damn about the future, except that they want power and they want money."

The "Pulliam people" is a reference to the major newspaper monopoly in Phoenix, the *Arizona Republic* and the *Phoenix Gazette*. Since Eugene C. Pulliam purchased the newspapers in the 1940s, they have become the most potent political and advertising force in the state. Though there are a few suburban dailies, the R&G (*Republic* and *Gazette*) is truly the big opinion-maker. Editorially Republican and conservative, the R&G is acknowledged as the spokesman for the business-oriented Arizona establishment.

The morning paper (the *Republic*) and the afternoon paper (the *Gazette*) have separate editorial staffs, but sales (advertising), the printing plant, and basic editorial policy are one and the same.

Despite notoriously low pay for some members of the editorial departments, the R&G has some excellent journalistic talent on the staffs who seem to be waging a continuous intra-office battle with management. At times, opinions expressed on the editorial page are diametrically opposed to the conclusions expressed in a page-one featured story.

But it is always constant, always faithful, in its defense of the state's power structure and its business establishment.

A lawyer and one of the top political leaders in Arizona expressed his opinion of the Pulliam press by saying, "Here is this vast organization with a 250,000 circulation with an opportunity to do so much good in this community, yet does so little. Instead we have a lack of leadership. We pay our legislators a lousy $6,000 a year because the paper screams all the time."

This Arizona leader holds the Pulliam press responsible for much of the state's bad reputation. "If the R&G had been on top of this, we wouldn't have had this lousy situation."

Matt Wheeler, current state chairman of the Democratic party in Arizona, also voiced his opinion. "This paper [R&G] is probably more responsible for what has happened than anything there is. They could take, make, or break anybody they wanted to. Anybody who disagreed with what they wanted was suddenly not around."

Another top state figure, Burton Barr, the Republican majority leader in the state House of Representatives, made some interesting comments on the policies of the Pulliam press in regard to investigative reporter Don Bolles.

For a number of years, the Pulliam press in Arizona

176

in conjunction with Congressman Sam Steiger carried on a campaign against the Emprise Corporation of Buffalo, New York. It was alleged that Emprise was "mob-connected" and was attempting a takeover of dog racing in the state. The R&G spearheaded by the investigative reporting of Don Bolles, went all-out in an effort to remove Emprise influence in Arizona.

Representative Barr offered his comment in this regard: "Don Bolles went all over the United States in an attempt to identify this problem. As to how successful he was, that has yet to be determined. I do know that Emprise went to the newspaper [*Arizona Republic*], and I think what I'm about to say is an important issue and should be brought out, but Don told me that at some point there was a meeting, and at some point he was told to 'lay back.' Now, I wasn't purview to that meeting, all I know is that at some point in his [Bolles'] investigation, Emprise was going to bring a suit against the paper or they did, and it was then that Bolles was either taken off the story or whatever."

Alone, without newspaper support, Sam Steiger upon leaving Congress also called off his campaign against Emprise, and asked the President to pardon the corporation for its alleged peccadillos.

Whatever its virtues and its vices the R&G is really the only game in town, and as a monopoly it has the power and the problems of a monopoly. There is a form of sibling rivalry between the staffs of the *Republic* and the *Gazette* in the gathering and reporting of news, but the hard-core editorial policy is the same for both.

The absence of newspaper competition and close ties with the business community have produced a management attitude that may be described as monopolistic. What the top echelon of the R&G deems proper for the community or the state is presented to its readers with an air of omniscience, and opposing points of view are relegated to relatively small articles buried deep on inside pages.

One individual, a well-known Republican lawyer and politician, has even voiced the theory that the management of the R&G may have had some conspiratorial connection with the actual death of Don Bolles. This usually reliable source explained this theory in the following words:

"Apparently the thought is that these old families, these people who have been around for a while, back in the forties and early fifties found that it was necessary in order to stimulate and control the growth of Phoenix, it was necessary to take control [of the power structure]. And it was probably well that they did. But they did what Nixon did and tried to cover up, and some of the things they did began to make them look like criminal conspirators. They still had good motives, but then people like Ned Warren came in, and they used people like Goldwater and Steiger and Rosenzweig, and duped them. And instead of admitting they were duped, they did what Nixon did and tried to cover up. And Pulliam was involved, Mason Walsh was involved, a lot of those people were involved directly, and the theory is that Bolles was getting too close to that—and that the newspaper is as guilty as anyone else in Bolles' death—and possibly Kemper Marley was a scapegoat because he was old and has all the earmarks of being the kind of guy that everyone would suspect and that they were just trumping it up on him."

When the late Eugene C. Pulliam took over the ownership of the *Arizona Republic* and the *Phoenix Gazette* on October 27, 1946, a creed to guide the publications was printed. In part this creed said, "The basic policy of these newspapers will be to continue to give Arizona the very best newspapers which the *Republic* and the *Gazette*'s fine family of employees can produce. The first duty of citizenship is useful service

178

to one's community. These newspapers want to be good citizens. The people of Arizona can count on them when there is worthy work of any sort to be done. Dedicated to a policy of common sense, common honesty, and common decency, these papers offer friendly and constructive cooperation to the churches, the schools, the civic organizations, the business institutions, the labor unions, the agricultural and other organizations of this state. Their columns will be open for discussion of civic, social, and political questions in signed contributions. They will strive always to be clean, broadminded, progressive, fair, helpful, patriotic, and *above all, truthful and accurate.*"

This creed was reaffirmed upon the death of publisher Eugene C. Pulliam on June 23, 1975, and signed by Nina Pulliam, publisher, and Mason Walsh, assistant publisher.

The noble purposes so eloquently expressed in the creed have at times seemed to be at cross-purposes with actual performance.

As mentioned by Republican state legislative leader Burton Barr, prudence was the best part of principle when the newspapers called off their lengthy campaign against the Emprise Corporation, which they had alleged was connected to the Mafia.

It has also been widely reported that the R&G's hierarchy discouraged its reporters from pursuing a story that would have proved embarrassing to the Valley National Bank, the state's largest. The story concerned a loss of $4 million to the Valley Bank through loans to C. Arnholt Smith, a San Diego, California, financier and former friend of President Nixon's. Other newspapers played the story big.

According to the *New York Times*, "Pat Murphy, the *Republic*'s editorial page editor, said that the controversy over the Valley National case was nothing more than a disagreement among editors and writers over its importance. In relation to the bank's total deposits, he said the $4 million was small. He compared it to 'making a case out of your friendly grocer stealing 25 cents.' "

R&G coverage after the death of Don Bolles was interesting. For several months, the *Republic* and the *Gazette* covered every aspect of the story, but then suddenly, the investigative probing of business interests connected to principals in the case stopped. Perhaps prosecutors were worried that the publicity would jeopardize their cases against suspects. Whatever the reason, the Bolles coverage was suddenly limited and largely confined to court actions.

However, refusing to print the series of investigative articles by the IRE (Investigative Reporters and Editors) not only dismayed but angered a considerable body of the R&G's readership. In a boxed front-page statement in the Sunday, March 13, 1977, *Arizona Republic* the R&G management said it was not going to run the IRE series because "Some of the previously unpublished material contains statements and allegations for which the *Republic* and the *Gazette* have not yet been able to obtain sufficient documentation and proof to justify publication."

Robert Greene of *Newsday*, who led the group of IRE reporters that prepared the series, is quoted in the *New York Times* as saying that the *Republic*'s decision "underlines what is terribly wrong with Phoenix and Arizona. People are not given an opportunity to know what's going on there."

A number of the nation's newspapers did not run the series as originally written, even though they had reporters who were participating in the project, but most of these papers said it was due to their lack of corroborating evidence. *Newsday,* Robert Greene's own paper, ran the series but deleted certain passages which they apparently felt lacked sufficient corroboration. Others ran it verbatim.

According to Robert Greene, all of the IRE files were copied by the R&G, which was not the case with many other newspapers which ran the stories or did not run them.

Just why the R&G did not have its lawyers blue-pencil the IRE material and run an edited version of the series remains an Arizona mystery.

Another mystery is the statement that was printed in the Sunday box announcing that the R&G would not run the series: "Copies of these articles [IRE series] also have been made to the *Arizona Republic*, although neither the *Republic* nor the *Phoenix Gazette* was a participant in the project."

It was well-known that the R&G *was* participating in the IRE project.

Robert Greene, who headed up the IRE team, is quoted as saying, "The *Republic* and its sister paper, the *Phoenix Gazette*, both owned by the Pulliam family, had offered the team the full use of their files and had provided office supplies and the services of three reporters, two of whom helped write the series."

The March 1977 issue of *The Quill*, a magazine of the Society of Professional Journalists, Sigma Delta Chi, an organization that Eugene C. Pulliam helped found in 1909, has an article entitled "The Arizona Squad," an inside story by Nina Bondarook. In this article there is a box listing the entire IRE group, and listed as representing the *Arizona Republic* are reporters John Winters, Mark Adams, and Chuck Kelly. Adams is listed as having worked exclusively as a writer on the team, and Robert J. Early, city editor of the *Arizona Republic*, is listed as assisting with liaison activities. Continuing with the following paragraph from the article: "Myrta Pulliam of the *Indianapolis Star* was at a disadvantage from the start. Her grandfather, the late Eugene C. Pulliam, had been publisher of (and her grandmother Nina still owns) the *Arizona Republic* and the *Phoenix Gazette*, with several other papers. Sometimes telephone tipsters hesitated to give the information to her when they heard her name. They said they felt the Phoenix papers had not done as much as possible in uncovering organized crime in the state."

Yet, the *Republic* says that it was *not* a participant in the project.

The people in Phoenix had to buy an out-of-town newspaper the *Arizona Star* (Tucson) in order to find out at least partially what the IRE reports said.

Even the tiny *Lake Havasu City Herald*, headed up by gutsy, intelligent young publisher-editor Joseph Soldwedel, had the courage to print the IRE exposé on Lake Havasu.

Chapter 10

THE ORGANIZATION

"Hey, kid!" he said in a husky whisper, "I've got a offer you can't refuse."

This famous line, which stemmed from the movie *The Godfather*, is symbolic of the image of an organized-crime figure that exists in all too many minds. This stereotype of an Italian-born gangster has been used as a whipping boy for illegal, immoral, and unethical business practices for much too long a time. Organized crime is universal, and its figures speak with many accents and drawls that have no Mediterranean origin.

Too often Arizonans, as well as the residents of other states, look for stereotype villains on which they can place the blame for their troubles and frustrations, and too often the news media and the entertainment media are all too willing to go along with these misconceptions.

Crime, if you get down to the basics, is simply one way for a human being to get what he wants. It's the law of the jungle, ruthless competition minus the limitation of rules. It's the animal predator surviving as an individual in a hostile existence.

Most crimes are for money, for money is the medium to acquire necessities of life, security, pleasure, and power.

Most honest labor is done for the same purposes!

The only difference between the criminal and the honest man is that the criminal is an example of undisciplined selfishness while the honest man has disciplined his actions for a more effective method of gratifying his selfishness. There is a lot of the criminal in all of us.

The point of this somewhat sophomoric philosophy is to establish a proper perspective in any analytical look at organized crime in Arizona. The organized-crime problems of this state are not based in one ethnic community, nor are they the simplistic product of a bunch of bad guys. Organized crime cannot be viewed in such black and white terms as good and evil; it must be analyzed in shades of gray.

Organized crime must have the assistance of the honest people of the state, consciously, unconsciously, or subconsciously, in order to operate.

This is why Arizona has become such a haven for crooks of various types; the good people of the state have furnished and are furnishing aid to the unethical, illegal, and immoral elements which either were born in Arizona or migrated here from elsewhere.

But even these unethical, illegal, and immoral elements are not all bad. Though darker than most on the gray scale, many of these people have also contributed much to the society they are continuing to rob. They pay their taxes, they contribute to churches, they try to give their children a decent education, and they may furnish honest employment to a substantial number of people.

The organized-crime figure in Arizona very often is a highly respected member of the community, and a social success. As a matter of fact, the organized-crime figure tries very hard to acquire the image of a good solid citizen. It is necessary to the unethical, illegal, and immoral way he makes his money.

This is the basic reason that the pitifully few hard-working law-enforcement officers in the state find it difficult to root out Arizona's major criminal elements.

In the Depression days of the thirties, the good people were often forced by circumstance to borrow money at exorbitant rates of interest from the only people with ready amounts of cash, the organized criminal element. In the 1970s, however, the criminal often finances his illegal ventures with loans from highly respectable financial institutions at reasonable rates of interest.

The acquisition of money has become far more sophisticated, and only where the financial return is obviously enormous, as in the trafficking in drugs, does the organized criminal chance illegal actions. The current criminal much prefers working within the system than without.

Another aspect in criminal behavior seldom considered by a stereotyping society is that the organized-crime figure doesn't view his actions as intrinsically wrong.

The con man sees his victim as a mark, a stupid, greedy person whom the con man has been able to outwit.

The pimp views prostitution as a service business that functions more efficiently on an organized basis, while the prostitute sees her profession as a profitable way to utilize her physical capabilities in the same fashion a professional athlete might look at the NFL.

The illegal gambler considers his illegality as a puritanical aberration of the state in which he resides, since there is nothing wrong with gambling in Las Vegas, Atlantic City, or at the local racetrack.

The drug trafficker like the bootlegger of old contends that he is merely supplying the demands of a large and growing market, and that individual abuse of drugs is not his problem.

Many other criminals such as embezzlers, car thieves, and other rip-off artists see their activities as merely sharing the wealth with those who can afford it, and besides, they justify, their victims are usually insured.

Even the hit man regards his profession as simply a hastening of the inevitable, and sees no horror in the demise of his victims.

The criminal considers himself as someone who has the courage to take the dangerous path of illegality for the potential of greater monetary rewards. How many of us so-called honest citizens haven't at one time or another said to himself, "I'd do it, if I only had the guts!"

It is in the aforementioned context that we can look at the crime problems of Arizona with some measure of objectivity.

As previously mentioned, organized crime is universal in its ethnic makeup, but it is also true that the organized-crime groups or "Mafia families" who are Sicillian or Italian in their origins could be considered the aristocracy in the field of illegal business. Through the loyalties engendered by their close relationships and blood ties, they have over the years been able to build and maintain their Cosa Nostras where other illegal organizations have flowered and died within a short period of time.

For any organization to exist under the adverse conditions of an organized-crime group, the loyalty factor is paramount. While simple greed or fear of punishment may be able to maintain some measure of discipline within an organization, and discipline is absolutely necessary, it can only be maintained for a relatively short period of time. To achieve discipline over the long haul, loyalty must spring from a feeling within that the interests of the organization are more important than the interests of any individual member.

It is for this primary reason that the mafiosi who migrated from Sicily have been able to create, maintain, and expand their organizations.

To understand the Mafia, one must understand the tremendous influence brotherhood plays in creating an almost fanatic loyalty among its members. To the true mafiosi, the organization or the family is sacred, and its survival is nearly a religion.

In political terms, it could be compared to such brotherhoods as the kamikazes of World War II or the extremist groups that have emerged from the Palestine Liberation Organization.

In a religious sense, the Mafia might well be compared to the brotherhood of the Mormon Church or the Black Muslim communities, not morally or ethically of course, but because of the fraternal emphasis extant in these groups.

It is said, however, that in recent years some of the old mafiosi traditions, rituals, and oaths have been de-emphasized by the younger, Americanized leadership that has taken over various family operations. Still, the close ties of blood and brotherhood exist within the family structure.

Contrary to popular belief, the Mafia or the Cosa Nostra is not a monolith. It is a loose federation of separate and distinct family organizations who form syndicates from time to time to further certain operations and businesses. There is no evidence to suggest that all the mafiosi families are subject to the control of one single council or leader.

The closest approximation to a current boss of bosses is Giuseppe Bonanno, better known to law-enforcement officials and the news media as Joe Bananas. He is the last surviving Mafia boss to have come to power at the creation of the modern Mafia in the United States in 1931. His official home since 1942 has been Tucson, Arizona. At seventy-two years of age, the appellation boss of bosses is probably more academic or emeritus than actual.

According to published reports, a former underboss in the Bonanno family, sixty-seven-year-old Carmine Galante, is emerging as a top figure in the New York area. These reports say that Galante has taken the place of Carlo Gambino in the Big Apple and is attempting to merge New York's five crime families into a single powerful group, and has aspirations to be the national boss of *all* mafiosi families.

Some knowledgeable people say, however, that Galante is still just a right arm to Joe Bonanno, and that his current takeover in New York is merely a holding action until Joe Bonanno's son, Salvatore "Bill" Bonanno, can acquire the knowledge and experience to step into the picture.

Carmine Galante was released from prison in 1974 after serving twelve years on a narcotics conviction. According to the *New York Times*, one federal agent said, "Galante used his twelve years in prison as a kind of health farm, building up his body with exercise and handball." Upon his release, it was said by the *Times* that the interim boss of Bonanno's New York family, Phillip Rastelli, eagerly handed control of the family over to Galante. It was also suggested that Galante had been meeting with and succeeded in winning the support of several other New York family bosses.

What is significant about Galante's push for control is his reported interest in expanding mafiosi control over the lucrative trafficking in hard drugs. Carlo Gambino, the most powerful Mafia leader in the 1960s, had steered the families away from the drug traffic, but Galante reportedly disagreed with Gambino, who died in the fall of 1976, and is now said to be setting up a narcotics network which has the backing of many of the Mafia's family leaders.

If the suppositions in these published reports are

correct, the effect on Arizona could be considerable. Arizona sits on the border of Mexico, and in recent days has acquired the reputation of being the drug corridor to the nation. Joe Bonanno lives in Tucson, just a hop, skip, and tumble from the border, and over the period since 1942 has built up contacts throughout the Arizona establishment. This all looks ominous for a state whose drug-enforcement programs have become political battlegrounds.

Yet, are these suppositions valid?

Is the Mafia really as wealthy, powerful, and effective as it once was?

A number of sources report that since the 1950s, most family money has been placed into legitimate business, and that direct operational activities in illegal areas have been generally abandoned. These sources say that independent entrepreneurs in illegal operations who have Mafia connections do borrow money at substantial rates of interest at times from family funding operations, but these are simply loans and the families are not involved in the actual illegal operations.

The Kefauver Committee in the 1950s reported the presence of known organized-crime figures in approximately fifty areas of business enterprise. These areas included: advertising, appliances, the automobile industry, banking, coal, construction, drugstores and drug companies, electrical equipment, florists, the food industry (such as meat, groceries, seafood, dairy products, cheese, olive oil, and fruits), the garment business, import-export, insurance, paper products, radio stations, ranching, real estate, restaurants, the scrap metal business, shipping, steel, television, theaters, and transportation.

Some say this concerted effort by the Mafia to penetrate legitimate business is merely an attempt to corrupt the businesses involved and milk them dry. Others believe the penetration is the real thing, that many of

189

the families, tired of being considered villains, have abandoned their old crude illegal ways and find it is more profitable to operate honest, legitimate business ventures.

Harry Rosenzweig, a Phoenix businessman and former state chairman of the Republican party in Arizona, is a man with considerable knowledge of what's going on in the Western United States, and he doesn't believe there is any extensive penetration of legitimate business by mafiosi in Arizona. He also says the "Bugsy Siegel days" are over in Las Vegas, and that with few small exceptions there is little mob ownership of the large hotels and gambling casinos.

Rosenzweig in an interview volunteered the following comment: "Just take a look at La Costa [a resort near San Diego, California], that's all Teamsters money and a place that all the gang leaders want to wind up their remaining years in peace and solitude. I don't think they're active today. I think they've got it [money] buried and want to live a quiet life. Moe Dalitz is alone, he wants to be recognized as a nice human being."

Moe Dalitz is a former Cleveland mobster who was known as a top behind-the-scenes man in the 1930s. In the late forties, Dalitz and some friends from Cleveland acquired controlling stock in the then new Desert Inn in Las Vegas. In the late sixties, Dalitz became a major stockholder in the Del Webb Corporation.

In discussing attempts by organized-crime figures to worm their way into the graces of Arizona's social elite, Harry Rosenzweig, who has long been considered one of the most influential men in the state, cited the case of Ned Warren, now affectionately known as "the godfather of Arizona land fraud."

Rosenzweig said, "When Ned Warren first came here, he presented money to the symphony and he was acclaimed as a real nice guy. He was very gracious, very well-dressed, and very mannered."

Rosenzweig continued, "I've only been with him twice in my life. When I told him I didn't want to go into business with him, that ended our friendship. He even agreed to loan me the money," Rosenzweig said, "but I told him I wasn't interested.

"He [Warren] told these reporters [IRE] that he knew me very well," Rosenzweig commented. "Everybody knows me very well! I can just meet somebody and suddenly I'm his best friend."

Another mafioso of some renown who is living in Arizona is Pete Licavoli, Sr. Now seventy-three years of age and in poor health, Licavoli was alleged to have been the leader of Detroit's infamous Purple Gang. He owns an 80-acre ranch near Tucson, and in recent years has reportedly made a fortune on his investments in the Las Vegas Strip, that famous boulevard lined with mammoth hotels and gambling casinos in Nevada's city of lights and losers.

Early in 1977, Licavoli was arrested and sentenced to eighteen months for trying to sell a hot painting to a federal agent.

The Mafia *are* in Arizona, of that there is no doubt.

Are they operating here? Are they into legitimate business here?

The answer to both questions is yes, but the extent is difficult to ascertain.

Joe Bonanno, for example, has described himself as a dealer in real estate, and reportedly operates in Arizona through a corporation known as Trans-West Trust, Inc. He is also into agriculture, and operated a cotton farm near Marana for many years. These are but a few of his local interests in business. As to whether he is operating as a part of organized crime is another matter.

In this regard, the so-called knowledgeable people in

and out of law enforcement voice opinions ranging from "complete retirement" to "dynamic leadership" of the nation's crime industry.

The wide discrepancy is partially due to a lack of knowledge, and partially due to what is known in Washington as "the annual Pentagon budget pitch" syndrome.

Local, state, and federal officials often exaggerate the activities of those labeled as organized-crime figures in order to pry loose larger appropriations for their respective departments. It's common practice. In addition, there are provincial jealousies between the various law-enforcement agencies which cause them to emphasize those areas with which the specific department or agency is most familiar or which offer the best potential for recognition and budgetary increases.

Even individual law-enforcement officers have a tendency to tell horror stories to gullible members of the news media for comparable reasons. This should be expected, since law-enforcement officers are members of a profession somewhat isolated from the rest of society. A cop's life isn't a bed of roses or a thirty-year supply of Kojak lollipops, and perhaps at times a craving develops for some recognition and empathy from the community he serves. So, as a natural consequence, he may exaggerate a bit here and there.

While experienced reporters on the police beat may suspect that some stories are exaggerated, if they are said by a usually reliable police source or provide interesting news copy, they usually are reported.

This presents a problem to the public at large. What *is* the *actual* status of crime in the community?

In Arizona, the situation can be described with reasonable accuracy as not too bad in some areas, and a national disgrace in others. Despite the irrational fears among some, particularly the elderly, most people can walk the streets of Arizona without getting mugged, raped, or murdered. Encanto Lagoon in Phoenix has not yet become a Central Park. But when it comes to white collar crime and the drug traffic, Arizona is now the cesspool of the world.

If the latter situation is to be changed, it will require a drastic reassessment of our city, county, state, and federal priorities, a flesh-colored Band-Aid won't help.

From the bottom to the top, such a reassessment must include a realization that organized crime is a multi-faceted problem and not the simplistic nonsense that's so regularly portrayed on our TV sets and motion picture screens.

Secondly, we must come to grips with the distasteful fact that it's going to take a major expenditure of our hard-earned dollars. A war is costly, and that's what's necessary, a war on crime.

A third item, and perhaps the most important, is that we *cannot* fight crime on one level and tolerate it at another. A pleasant, smiling con man with a cute wife and kiddies and a card in the noontime Rotary Club is just as much a criminal as some black teenager who wields a Saturday night special in a supermarket.

One Arizonan, because of his background and current influential position, is uniquely qualified to discuss the problems and answers in the field of white collar and organized crime. He is the state's newest member of the United States Senate, Dennis DeConcini.

A native of Tucson, DeConcini is a member of a wealthy politically oriented family who have been influential in the state for many years. His mother, Mrs. Ora DeConcini, is a Democratic party activist who currently is Democratic national committeewoman from the state of Arizona. His father, Evo DeConcini, is a former Arizona Supreme Court justice, Arizona attorney general, Pima County Superior Court judge, and state democratic chairman. His brother, Dino DeConcini, is presently executive assistant to Governor Raul Castro.

At forty years of age, Senator Dennis DeConcini is a lawyer with experience in both sides of the legal arena, as a prosecutor and as a defense attorney in the law firm of DeConcini and McDonald.

Politically active since 1958, he has served in a number of capacities within the Democratic party of Arizona. He was employed on the state level as special counsel to former Arizona governor Sam Goddard, and later became the governor's administrative assistant. In November 1972, DeConcini was elected Pima county attorney. Concurrent with his duties as Pima county attorney, he was appointed administrator of the Arizona Drug Control District by Governor Raul Castro.

In November of 1976, he defeated the Republican nominee, former U. S. Congressman Sam Steiger, for the U. S. Senate seat which had been occupied by former Arizona governor and U. S. senator Paul Fannin.

In addition to these qualifications, however, is another. As a resident of Tucson, right smack dab in the middle of Arizona's Mafia country, U. S. Senator Dennis DeConcini is also the product of Italian ancestry. Politically, it's not a comfortable position, and the young freshman senator from Arizona knows full well that he is under the proverbial microscope. Though obviously intelligent, competent, and personable, there are many in the state who continue to ask the question brought up during his recently successful Senate campaign; "Is he or isn't he the Mafia's man in Washington?"

"No!" he answers vehemently.

Yet, in the glare of the state's current reputation, the question lingers.

Though Arizona rejected Democrat Jimmy Carter in November of 1976, the voters were clearly willing to give this new Italian-American face on the national political scene a chance. Some say the election of Dennis DeConcini to the Senate is perhaps the most fortunate political occurrence that could have happened to the state. They reason DeConcini has only three avenues to go in an approach to organized crime; he can fight it, ignore it, or aid it. And most believe he will fight it.

Why the suspicion in the first place? Well, as mentioned, he's from Tucson, he's Italian, he's wealthy, he's an attorney, and he is a well-backed politician. In today's opinion market, the latter three reasons are sufficient for suspicion.

There are other factors. In 1954, Senator DeConcini's father, former Arizona Supreme Court Justice Evo DeConcini, testified as a defense character witness when the government tried to deport Joe Bonanno back to Sicily. Several other prominent Arizonans also testified on Bonanno's behalf, but Judge DeConcini was obviously the most influential of the lot.

Senator DeConcini explains his father's testimony by saying that Judge DeConcini was "subpoenaed" to testify and had no other course but to make the appearance at the hearing. Since his father could only testify to what he personally knew, the only way it could come out was in Bonanno's favor. This was true, he said, because Judge DeConcini could only testify as to Joe Bonanno's reputation and activities in Tucson, where he had maintained a pure and benevolent behavior.

Some say, however, that the judge's words at the hearing were too enthusiastic.

In Tucson, Joe Bonanno had from the time he arrived there in 1942 set about to become a respected member of the community. He gave an organ to a Catholic church in the city, it is said, and did everything possible to ingratiate himself with Tucson's social elite. So it is possible that Judge DeConcini actually

195

believed Bonanno to be the good citizen his local activities suggested.

Whether it was honest conviction, a lack of knowledge, or something else that prompted the words in the testimony, its effect carries to the present.

Most Arizonans do not believe the sins of a father should carry to the son, or so they say, but it does make them wary.

Another problem in this regard cropped up during Senator DeConcini's campaign. A number of contributions came in from people with alleged mob connections, and he was asked by his opponent Sam Steiger to explain them. DeConcini said that some of the questioned contributions had been returned, others would be returned, and some that he had personally investigated would be kept.

A $50 contribution from Victor Tronolone was returned. Tronolone has many times been identified as an accountant for Joe Bonanno and Peter Licavoli, Mafia chieftains.

A $175 contribution by Tucson smoke shop operator Michael Cosenza was returned. Cosenza's daughter's wedding reportedly attracted a number of mob figures including Salvatore Spinelli, Joseph Bonanno, Jr., and Charles Battaglia.

Two other contributions from alleged mob-connected figures were kept, a $1,000 contribution from Tucson developer Sam Nanini, and a $250 contribution from Tucson banker John Chiapetta.

The senator explained his reasons for doing this in an interview.

"I did an in-depth background search of Nanini years ago and found nothing I could possibly see in any criminal connection," DeConcini said. "He comes from Chicago," the senator continued, "and I could not find out all of the dealings and contracts that he had been involved in back there, but he's been in Arizona for some twenty-five or thirty years now, and in Arizona there is just absolutely nothing that would taint his record." DeConcini also volunteered the information that his law office had represented Nanini on several occasions.

Regarding the Chiapetta contribution, Senator DeConcini said, "It was mentioned that John Chiapetta once had lunch with Bonanno or Licavoli, or one of those guys, and there was some discussion about the sale of land. Well," the senator said, "I've known him all my life, and the fact that he had thought about selling land to an identifiable underworld character is not involving him [in criminal activities]. In this case, he didn't go ahead and sell it," DeConcini remarked.

The mere fact that some mob figures wanted to contribute indicated to some that there must be a connection.

What is often forgotten, if realized in the first place, is that members of the Mafia or other groups in organized crime are made up of a cross section of people who have many interests besides making money illegally. Believe it or not, some are scholars, some deeply religious, and some are interested in politics in a general sense, as well as its uses to further mob activities. Some are Republicans and some are Democrats with political philosophies as widely diverse as the general population. As a result, individual mobsters will make contributions for many reasons besides the obvious one of corruption.

If the Mafia wanted to buy a politician, it is doubtful that they would permit their well-known members to make contributions in their own names. Common sense says they would either use aliases or give it through other individuals with clean names. They would not give their stooge's opponent election ammunition.

Political professionals well acquainted with campaign practices say it's a common dirty trick to suggest and prove during a campaign that your opponent is backed by unpopular or illicit interests. On the other hand, these professionals say a more sophisticated approach using reverse psychology is for a candidate actually to solicit contributions from unsavory characters in order to give the impression that an opponent *is using* dirty tricks.

Whether any of the above political gimmicks were applied in DeConcini's 1976 campaign remains a matter of conjecture.

Those who believe DeConcini will *be* a crime fighter say that because of his Italian background, he is more anxious than most to prove that all Italians are *not* mafiosi.

Senator DeConcini, in response to the question, "How do you tell the good Italians from the bad Italians?" said, "I don't know the answer, except to look at the record of people. An example, Judge Sirica has got to be a good Italian, if you want to classify him as Italian. He has had the courage to take on Italian interests in his court and sit on those cases, and of course, he's the one that stood up to the executive in a very abusive situation."

Judge Sirica is famous for his decisions and actions during Watergate.

Senator DeConcini, who prior to his election was Pima county attorney and administrator of a four-county drug strike force, frankly admits that the major portion of the drug traffic through Arizona is conducted by the Mafia and other family-type organizations.

"We believe that as much as 60 per cent [drug traffic] is tied to organized crime, some of which is the Mafia, that is, Italian-heritage families, and Mexican-American families which operate in the same tradition as the Italian types."

"What are *you* doing to battle organized crime?" DeConcini was asked.

"Well, there are a couple of things brewing. First of all, Governor Raul Castro and myself have gone to see Attorney General Griffin Bell, and there are good indications that he is going to send a substantial increase in the personnel of the U. S. District Attorney's office, both investigators and attorneys who will be designated to work on white-collar and organized crime as well as narcotics," he said.

"In addition to that," DeConcini continued, "Governor Castro along with the governors of New Mexico, Colorado, and Utah at my suggestion have filed a grant application with the LEAA [Law Enforcement Assistance Administration] for a four-state regional narcotics intelligence network."

DeConcini says that previous federal efforts to combat organized crime have been cosmetic, and cited Arizona as an example of the neglect by previous administrations.

"There are only twenty-eight or twenty-nine federal deputy district attorneys in Arizona," he said, "and that's a very, very small amount.

"When you think of the quantity of drug cases alone, plus civil jurisdiction for federal agencies, we have not had.[in Arizona] anything but a cosmetic approach to really combat organized crime and narcotics," DeConcini explained.

The new U. S. Attorney for Arizona, Mike Hawkins, revealed that his office had handled over fourteen hundred cases in 1976, two hundred of which went to trial. This case load was carried by twenty-five deputy attorneys. Other districts with comparable case loads have far more attorneys, he said. New York has over one hundred and Los Angeles has ninety.

As to his opinions on the efforts being made within the state itself to fight white collar and organized crime, Senator DeConcini has criticized the State Legislature for not passing anti-crime legislation, and said

199

the recent establishment of a state grand jury and the authorization of the four-county narcotics strike force are the only two positive measures it has taken.

DeConcini also lashed out at the Arizona Bar Association for its failures to police the state's legal profession, and to support tough anti-crime legislation.

When asked for a comment on the anti-crime efforts of fellow Democrat Arizona Attorney General Bruce Babbitt, DeConcini mused, "Whether or not Bruce will succeed will depend on whether or not he wants to be a real tiger—for it's tough, and you have to take on some sacred cows. I kind of think he's going to," DeConcini opined, "but we've yet to see it."

Chapter 11

THE EMPRISE FIASCO

As investigative reporter Don Bolles lay mangled but conscious beside his little white Datsun, he was heard by several people to mutter "Emprise" and "Mafia."

Phoenix fireman Mark Flick is quoted as saying, "While I was down there by him, he said if he doesn't make it, he wanted us to know that this was an assassination by the Mafia."

This belief voiced by the dying reporter was the result of nearly seven years of work by Bolles in his attempt to tie the Emprise Corporation, a sports concession conglomerate headquartered in Buffalo, New York, to organized crime. Don was a logical person, and it's easy to understand that as he lay sprawled on the dirt of the hotel parking lot, he would reach the conclusion of his statement.

Who else had been the subject of his journalistic barbs for such a long period of time?

Who else commonly used bombing as a method of assassination?

He obviously knew that John Adamson had set him up for the bombing attack, and if there is anyone in this world that looks the part of a stereotyped hood it's Adamson.

In Don's mind, the pieces fit.

Exactly how and when the attacks on Emprise Corporation activities began is somewhat vague in the memories of those involved, but a consensus agrees that the initial probing started in the late 1960s.

Emprise Corporation was established in Buffalo, New York, in 1961 to act as a holding company for a number of corporate activities that grew from a small peanut-selling company called Jacobs Brothers founded in 1915. Sons of an immigrant Polish tailor who moved to Buffalo at the turn of the century, the Jacobs brothers, Charley, Marvin, and Louie, hawked peanuts, popcorn, and hot dogs at sporting events or wherever they could set up a profitable concession. It was the youngest brother, Louie, who apparently had the drive and chutzpah to make this business succeed, and succeed it did. In 1927, the firm got its first concession contract to dispense food and drink at a major-league baseball park with the Detroit Tigers.

While the concession business was lucrative, Louie Jacobs was sharp enough to loan money from time to time to ailing baseball franchises and acquired a good rapport with the owners and operators. This in turn produced more concession contracts permitting an expansion of his concession business. The Jacobs Brothers company not only expanded but diversified. It was eventually able to buy ownership in the sports franchises themselves.

By 1961, the concession business name had been changed to Sportservice, and due to Jacobs participation in a number of other corporations, the Emprise holding company was deemed necessary.

In 1972, Emprise reportedly furnished food and drink to the fans at seven major-league baseball parks, serviced eight professional football teams, five professional basketball teams, and four hockey franchises. In addition, it had an ownership in a variety of sports franchises, and is said to have had stocks, bonds, and debentures in at least nineteen pari-mutuel operations such as horse racing, dog racing, and jai alai.

Its Sportservice segment was able to grab the food and drink concession at the 1960 Olympic games in Rome, Italy, quite a feat in food-conscious Europe.

In the early 1970s, Emprise reportedly admitted to a total of 162 different companies within its overall structure, and its total value was said to be enormous, with Sportservice alone grossing $100 million a year. Needless to say, Emprise Corporation was big business, and much of its business resulted from Louie Jacobs' policy of making loans to the right people at the right time, particularly those involved in or around the professional sports industry.

One such loan made by the elder Louie Jacobs prior to his death in 1968 created the *cause célèbre* which his two sons, Jeremy and Max, and the corporation they head have had to battle in court, in Congress, in state hearings, and in the news media. This loan, it was alleged, demonstrated close ties between the Emprise Corporation and the Mafia.

Former Arizona congressman Sam Steiger recalls how investigative reporter Don Bolles in following up a story on dog racing in Arizona became interested in the Emprise Corporation, which operated the concessions at all the state's dog tracks, from information he received on an investigation of Emprise goings-on in Arkansas.

"As I recall, it was one of the dog owners who brought the story of the Arkansas investigator to Don, and that's what got Don interested," Steiger related.

Steiger, a Republican congressman and state legislator for many years, knew and worked intimately with Don Bolles on the Emprise effort in Arizona.

As to the story that apparently triggered Bolles' interest in the matter, Steiger remarked, "Don checked that out, and indeed, the Arkansas state police had had an investigator do some research on Emprise in Arkansas, and when it came time for him [the investigator] to testify before whatever body, he went to the hospital. To the best of my knowledge, he [the investigator] has never been heard of since," Steiger added, "and the report disappeared."

According to Steiger, Bolles had done a series of articles on dog racing in Arizona prior to getting wind of the Arkansas story.

It was well-known at the time that Eugene Pulliam, publisher of the *Arizona Republic* and *Gazette*, had no great love for the Funk family, who actually owned most of Arizona's dog tracks. Whether it was some bias toward the Funk family in particular or just dog racing per se that generated this feeling of animosity is not clearly understood. But it was evident that the Phoenix newspapers could not see Arizona "going to the dogs."

The Emprise Corporation originally was nothing more than a concession operator at the tracks, but when the Funks got into financial difficulties, Emprise came up with one of its famous Jacobs loans, thus increasing its clout on operation of the tracks.

The Arkansas story apparently intrigued the powers-that-be at the R&G after Bolles passed it on to management, for Don was authorized to go on an investigative tour of the various states in which Emprise was active. Bolles traveled all over the country digging out the details of Emprise's activities and operations, then returned to Phoenix, where he wrote a series of articles based on his trip.

"The articles had just barely started," Sam Steiger recalled, "when Burton Barr [state legislator] came to me, and in the course of our conversation, he explained to me that he was really upset about the dog tracks because a lawyer named George Hill who had hired on as

204

a legislative assistant had *really* hired on to pass some legislation for the dog tracks."

Steiger said this legislation was "not only favorable to the dog tracks but detrimental to the state, because they used a false profit and loss statement to show that they were losing money."

Sports Illustrated magazine in a lengthy article in May of 1972 said that the young lawyer in question "had received a legal fee from Emprise," and suggested or implied that the fee was for his influence in helping to pass the dog track legislation.

Steiger, then a congressman, said that state Representative Burton Barr and state Auditor General Ira Osman requested federal assistance in the matter, which he promised to give. As a politician, Congressman Sam Steiger was no doubt aware of the newspaper's apparent dislike of the dog track situation, and had the savvy to realize that being on the side of the angels with newspaper backing was potentially good for a political career. So when reporter Don Bolles approached Steiger with material he had gathered on Emprise and the dog tracks, the congressman was understandably receptive.

"Bolles brought me what was really the unpublished results of his trip around the country, and it was kind of fascinating," Steiger said. "And then, almost at the same time, the SEC [Securities and Exchange Commission] people brought me the documentation that Emprise was in partners with the Zerilli family in Detroit at the Hazel Park racetrack up there."

Anthony J. Zerilli of Detroit had been labeled by the McClellan Committee in Congress as a member of the Detroit Mafia.

Shortly after the Bolles series of articles and Sam Steiger's interest in the matter became public, the congressman was called to testify at a hearing on Emprise activities in New Mexico.

Ex-congressman Steiger relates, "The state of New Mexico was having a real problem with Emprise, their Racing Commission was, and they asked me to testify, so with my background from Bolles and the federal agencies, I laid out just what I thought Emprise was."

On March 4, 1970, Congressman Sam Steiger read into the *Congressional Record* a speech titled "Emprise: A Lesson in Corporate Calumny." In it he charged Emprise with being riddled with corruption, using its corruptive influence to gain concession advantages, hidden and overt control of sports franchises throughout the nation, and the big pitch that it worked hand in hand with organized crime.

Steiger, who was never known in Arizona as a shrinking violet, named various people who had a public reputation as members of the Mafia or organized crime, and listed their alleged associations with Emprise and the Jacobs family.

In addition to Anthony Zerilli, Steiger said the Hazel Park racetrack near Detroit had on its board of directors "Jack" Tocco, who also had been labeled as a Mafia figure by the McClellan Committee. Since Emprise at the time was said to own about 12 per cent of the track resulting from a Louie Jacobs loan to Zerilli and Tocco, Steiger cited this as an example of an Emprise tie-in with organized crime.

Jeremy and Max Jacobs counterattacked and said that Steiger was dragging out old business transactions that had occurred when they were still in school, and accused the congressman of using invalid guilt by association tactics. Both Zerilli and Tocco had never been convicted of a crime, they suggested, and Jacobs' attorney, Arnold Weiss, reportedly described Zerilli and Tocco as fine people.

Kefauver Committee hearings in the 1950s had produced testimony that Zerilli and Pete Licavoli, a current resident of Arizona, were members of the notorious

Purple Gang in Detroit which controlled organized crime in the early 1930s.

Emprise attorneys pointed out that Louie Jacobs' "loan" was made to a public company, and that Hazel Park racetrack was licensed by the SEC, with twelve hundred stockholders, and was under the jurisdiction of the Michigan State Racing Commission. Emprise also mentioned that the Buffalo company had been restructured and the old Emprise was no more.

Steiger reportedly admitted privately that most of his case against Emprise was based on guilt by association, but he lacked investigative resources to go further, and hoped that he could make enough noise to stimulate other official investigations in depth. Asked if he had any official congressional support when he launched his attack on the floor of Congress, Steiger replied, "No, this was just all ad hoc, it was 'Don Quixote' Steiger taking off at them."

The result of Steiger's charges was a sudden rash of hearings by racing commissions and crime commissions in five of the states where Emprise operations existed—New Mexico, Florida, Arkansas, Louisiana, and Arizona. The end product of these hearings, however, was simply bad publicity for Emprise and no criminal charges. The publicity also stimulated the Justice Department and the IRS to begin investigations on possible anti-trust and labor law violations, or whatever.

For a period of two years, there were all sorts of allegations from both sides but nothing substantial emerged. Then on April 26, 1972, a federal jury convicted six persons and one corporation of criminal conspiracy to obtain secret ownership of the Frontier casino-hotel in Las Vegas, Nevada. Among the six persons was Anthony Zerilli and Michael Polizzi, reputed Detroit mobsters, and the one corporation was Emprise.

It was a blow to the large Buffalo conglomerate, but not a fatal one.

As mentioned, after Louie Jacobs' death, the whole structure of the business was rearranged. Sportsystems, Inc., was established as the parent company, with Emprise being relegated to a subsidiary status. Emprise assets were sold or transferred to other corporations owned by the Jacobs family such as Ramcorp, a steel company. For example, all of Arizona's horse and dog racing interests owned by Emprise were transferred to Ramcorp, and other Emprise assets became a part of Arizona Sportservice, a direct subsidiary of Sportsystems, Inc.

The second blow came in May of 1972, when *Sports Illustrated* magazine printed a ten-page feature story by John Underwood and Morton Sharnik entitled "Look What Louie Wrought."

Horace Webb, an executive with Sportsystems, Inc., in Buffalo, declared, "That article was, of course, devastating as far as the Jacobses were concerned. The front page of the *Sports Illustrated* magazine," Webb continued, "carried a picture of Louie Jacobs, framed in an old-time frame, and the headline right across the top of the page was 'The Godfather of Sports.'"

The article was in essence a compendium of the various charges made by Sam Steiger and others prior to that time. It did feature seven photographs of alleged mobsters who had had some connection with Emprise, and stressed the allegations that the firm was apparently dealing with members of the so-called Mafia.

"We've been trying to live that down ever since," Webb stated.

From the article, and other published sources, it is clearly established that the phenomenal growth of the Emprise conglomerate over the years, regardless of its possible dealings with reputed mobsters, was the result of being a banker to franchises and ownerships in professional sports who found it difficult to get financing from conventional sources.

Reportedly there are eleven major concessionaires in the United States, and ARA Services, Inc., is said to be the largest overall, but among concessionaires who specialize in sports, Sportservice, a branch of Sportsystems, Inc., is considered number one. Other firms in direct competition with Sportservice are: Stevens, ABC Consolidated, Canteen Corporation, and Servomation.

Most of these sports concessionaires get into the private banking business in some fashion or other, for the simple reason that when a sports franchise collapses or a racetrack shuts down, or are not living up to their economic potentials due to a lack of expansion capital, the concessionaires also lose. So, in this regard, Sportsystems, Inc. (Emprise), is not unique.

As *Sports Illustrated* mentioned in its article, "The secret of growth in the concession business, however, is how well you use the contract-loan combination," and the magazine suggested that Louie Jacobs was a master in this field.

Horace Webb of Sportsystems, Inc., commented, "It's been recently upheld in the Supreme Court that loaning money to individuals in return for business considerations is permissible, and that's what Jacobs was castigated for these last four or five years."

Actually, most criticism is not based on the fact that loans were made, it is based primarily on to *whom* they were made.

There is a general and widespread belief that professional sports, and pari-mutuel sports in particular, are an irresistible attraction to certain elements of organized crime. Even though the franchises and the racetracks may be as pure as the driven snow, most illegal gambling is based on professional sports and racetracks. As a consequence, those who are connected in any way with professional sports or the racetracks are

209

most vulnerable to criticism regarding their associations, even innocent ones, with recognized figures in organized crime. If a grocer is seen talking to a known mafioso, that is one thing, but if a jockey or a racing judge is seen doing the same thing, that's another matter.

While there has been no public evidence that Sportsystems, Inc., has been owned or controlled by organized criminal elements, the mere fact that it is huge and successful suggests to some that it may have reached some live and let live accommodation with the powers that lurk in the underworld.

Something seldom mentioned, however, is the Buffalo firm's competition. Why? It hardly seems logical that in a lucrative, highly competitive business that deals in loans and contracts, the competition could even exist unless it used essentially the same tactics and dealt with the same people.

Since former Arizona congressman Sam Steiger has been the firm's most visible antagonist over the years, spokesmen for Emprise have asked, "Was public service the only motives for the Steiger attacks?"

Walter Cheifitz, an attorney representing Sportsystems, Inc., in Arizona, says the answer to this question has been the subject of investigative efforts by the Jacobs family. They wanted to find out, he said, "what made Sammy run."

Cheifitz explained that when Louie Jacobs died leaving his extensive business empire, the wolves descended with all sorts of accusations and tried to take it away from his sons.

"We have some leads," Cheifitz continued, "and we have a suit pending against a major competitor who was definitely behind a lot of it. It may be a whole combination of people who were interested in Jacobs family businesses that they felt they could acquire," he suggested.

"One we have confirmed," Cheifitz said, "and that's Servomation, now the subject of a large damage suit."

The suit in question also involves Congressman Steiger and a former aide, Michael Jarvis, both of whom were charged with conspiring to damage Emprise so that its concession contracts would be terminated, after which they would be awarded to the competitor, Servomation Dutchess Corporation of Delaware. Evidence presented in court suggested that Steiger had accepted campaign contributions from Hal Nunn, a former executive for Servomation, and from Murray Kemp, a racetrack owner in Oregon who donated in Nunn's name.

Attorney Cheifitz elaborated, "This man had been a former associate with the Jacobs family's businesses, and even worked for them for a while. Then he obtained employment by convincing Servomation that he was in a position to take business away [from Emprise]."

On the other side of the fence, Sam Steiger countersued the Emprise Corporation, and alleged that the Buffalo firm wiretapped his phone calls and hired persons to compile a smear file on him.

However, the campaign against Emprise has come to a screeching halt in the state of Arizona. After seven years of investigative reporting by Bolles and others, Sam Steiger's efforts in Congress, the *Sports Illustrated* article, and a host of hearings and investigations, it has stopped, just simply stopped.

Sam Steiger in a recent interview suggested some reasons for the collapse of the anti-Emprise crusade, described his last lengthy discussion with a disheartened Don Bolles, and gave his reaction to the suggestion that persons in the hierarchy of the *Republic* and *Gazette* were responsible for the reporter's death:

INTERVIEWER: Then you don't give any credence

211

to the theory that Bolles was on to something involving the newspaper?

STEIGER: That's crazy! In the first place, Bolles wasn't on to *anything*! The reason I say that is 'cause it wasn't four months before he was killed that we had a long talk in which he begged me to lay off Emprise 'cause nobody gave a damn . . . and it was no use to expose *anything* 'cause nobody cared.

INTERVIEWER: But wasn't the paper putting pressure on him to stay off the Emprise thing because there was a suit involved there?

STEIGER: Hey! The paper made a deal with Emprise. Don had to make a deal with Emprise; you see, Don was sued too! And the basis of the resolution of that suit was that they would lay off—and the paper will deny that to this day . . . and they're lying—just flat lying! They made a deal that they would lay off of Emprise, period! Hey, that's how Emprise—believe me, I know whereof I speak! They sued the *Arkansas Gazette* for 20 million, they sued the *Detroit Free Press* for 20 million, and they sued *Sports Illustrated*.

INTERVIEWER: That's a technique some people use, if they've got money, to drive other people into the ground economically over lawsuits.

STEIGER: Hey! That's what happened to me. It's no secret I could have kept my lawsuit going—in fact it still is going, as far as I know. But I'm looking at sixty thousand dollars in bills I owe, and I'm looking at another hundred thousand before this thing is over—and for what? Sure, I win, but I don't get any money, and in the meantime I don't have that kind of money.

No, that's a technique—that's right! It's called intimidation by legal process and it's very real.

That's what the paper was a victim of—and that's what Bolles himself was a victim of!

And Bolles—really—was tired of harassment. He didn't want any more of it, and I *know* that! Sure, he was a firehorse, if somebody rang a bell in his ear, he'd go respond, but—as far as him being on to something, I can't say he wasn't, but I know he wasn't looking. That is just nonsense!

INTERVIEWER: I have a feeling that the real villain of the piece, here in Arizona and perhaps throughout the country, is the legal profession.

STEIGER: Ahh! You have driven your ducks to the right market! I am firmly convinced that the attitude of the legal profession, and there are obviously excellent people in the legal profession—

INTERVIEWER: Oh, sure!

STEIGER: But! I *blame* them 'cause they don't clean up their own house . . . and the whole process, the whole litigatory process, civil and criminal, has become a function of "victory"—and justice is a victim in this thing.

This interview was made *after* the former congressman from Arizona had met with executives of Sportsystems, Inc., in Buffalo shortly after his defeat for the U. S. Senate in 1976. What was discussed at that meeting has not been revealed by either Steiger or Sportsystems, Inc., but in January of 1977, Sam Steiger confirmed to the news media that he had written to President Ford's Attorney General, Edward Levi, in December of 1976 requesting *approval* of a presidential pardon application made by Sportsystems, Inc., to expunge the felony conviction of conspiring to conceal its interests in a Las Vegas casino-hotel.

Steiger had written an earlier letter *opposing* the same application on the grounds that he suspected Emprise had illegally supported his primary opponent, former congressman John Conlan, and was continuing its associations with organized crime.

When asked to comment on his turnaround, Steiger said after an FBI probe of allegations contained in the letter opposing the application, he learned that the "source of our information about campaign contributions was just plain wrong." He also said that law-enforcement sources told him that Emprise had "busted its behind to get rid of the hoods in their outfit."

Steiger was also quoted as saying, "I don't think it's inconceivable to think that my efforts and the efforts of other people have convinced Emprise to clean up its act. And I think they've been successful at it."

In Arizona, Steiger's action was a shocker, to say the least.

Neither Steiger nor Sportsystems, Inc., would comment on whether a "deal" was made in Buffalo.

On January 25, 1977, it was reported that the million-dollar lawsuit against Sam Steiger had been suspended "indefinitely." A suspended suit is not the same as being dropped entirely; to all intents and purposes it's dead, but like the phoenix it can rise again from its own ashes.

On January 26, 1977, the *Arizona Republic* in an editorial that some say "smacks of the pot calling the kettle black" attacked Steiger's action.

YOU MUST BE KIDDING, SAM! was the editorial's headline. It continued by saying:

Sam Steiger has been called the best stand-up comedian in Arizona politics. But he has outdone himself in explaining why he wrote the U.S. Atorney General seeking a pardon for his old enemy, Emprise Corporation. Or maybe he's only kidding.

Emprise, if you've forgotten, was co-owner of the six Arizona dog tracks. Not so long ago it transferred its holdings in the tracks to Ramcorp Metals, Inc., the present owner.

Steiger, who apparently prefers horse tracks to dog tracks, had a running feud with Emprise when he was a member of Congress. Because Emprise was convicted of conspiracy in a federal court, Steiger said, "It is is very important to throw them [Emprise] out. Otherwise Arizona will be viewed as welcoming hoodlums."

The editorial continued and called Steiger's letter approving the pardon "the greatest about-face since Corrigan flew the wrong way across the Atlantic." It wound up by facetiously suggesting that Steiger's reason for approving the pardon was to get his lawsuit dropped, and ended with the comment, "Politics and dog tracks make strange bedfellows."

The application for the pardon was made by Sportsystems, Inc., in August 1975, and reportedly was expected to take at least eighteen months to process.

Seven years have passed since Steiger began his attacks. Seven years filled with invective, investigations, and inefficacy. What has been accomplished?

On the surface, the answer would be—nothing.

Emprise, restructured, continues to operate. Out of the host of revelations and investigations, not one single official or employee of the Buffalo firm has been indicted, tried, or jailed for a crime. In the one instance where the corporation was found guilty of conspiracy, its number-one antagonist has requested a presidential. pardon.

It would be easy to say that the crusade against the Emprise Corporation was either the greatest injustice that has ever been perpetrated on a single American business firm, or a testimonial that it is impossible to combat the entrenched influence of organized crime. But reality probably exists somewhere in between.

Don Bolles believed that Emprise was corrupt, and in a sense he was undeniably correct, for who among us is not corrupt? The problem is in determining the extent of corruption, and therein lies the hassle of ambiguity.

As mentioned earlier, the preponderance of evidence suggesting Emprise's connections with organized crime was accumulated by the technique known as guilt by association. Properly used, this technique is a valuable and necessary tool in uncovering the hidden dangers that may exist in a society. Yet it is truly a dangerous thing, for like optical glass it has a tendency either to help us see things more clearly, or to distort and magnify reality if shaped for that purpose. Quite similar to the polling techniques used in politics and marketing, associative indictment must not stem from prejudging, and must be based on a sufficient sample.

In assessing the testimony and published allegations against the Emprise Corporation, one must first determine if the material was investigative reporting, advocacy journalism, or a historic critique.

One justifiable complaint from Sportsystems, Inc., is that if there were past sins, the sins of the father should not be blamed on his sons. If Louie Jacobs loaned money to unsavory individuals, or in any way aided elements of organized crime, these incidents are of historical significance only. What should be important to investigators, journalistic or otherwise, is whether there are any current connections between Emprise and the criminal underworld.

What is the current status of Sportsystems, Inc. (formerly Emprise)?

Their old antagonist Sam Steiger says they have cleaned up their act.

The defense attorneys for Max Dunlap say they will contend in court that Phoenix attorney Neal Roberts

216

set up the Bolles bombing to benefit the Funk greyhound racing circuit and the Emprise Corporation.

The Emprise story in Arizona has not as yet reached a conclusion, but will anyone in the state have the intestinal fortitude to tell it?

Since 1970, Sportsystems, Inc., of Buffalo, New York, has developed a small army of legal talent to defend itself. This is understandable. But their recent successes in silencing opposition through what has been termed "intimidation by legal process" are rather frightening.

Many supposed stalwarts have had to knuckle under.

Chapter 12

THE IRE REPORTS

"We are reporters. We cannot deny the solidarity that must exist between us, or we're all going to get picked off." This statement attributed to Robert Greene of the Long Island newspaper *Newsday* apparently served as the rationale for the establishment of something new and unique in journalism, the investigative group.

As a direct result of the Bolles bombing, the IRE (Investigative Reporters and Editors), an organization of which Don Bolles was a member, began the formation of what was to be called the Arizona Project.

While pooled reports have been common to wartime reporting, the establishment of a group of professional journalists, with no ties to each other save their profession, to investigate and report on a single area of inquiry had never been attempted.

The stated purpose in the formation of this unique investigative group was "to advance as much as possible the investigative work started by Bolles and to symbolize as dramatically as possible the resolve of the communications media to be even more perseverant in the search for truth in the face of threats of physical harm to a reporter."

Funded by donations from the Arizona Association of Industries, participating newspapers, television stations, radio stations, and others, the IRE recruited the services of over forty reporters and editors from twenty-eight participating news organizations and put together an investigative group which would probe the status of crime in the state of Arizona and write a series of articles on the results of the investigation.

Among the participating news organizations were: *Albuquerque Journal, Arizona Daily Star, Boston Globe,* CBS/WEEI Boston, *Chicago Tribune, Colorado Springs Sun, Denver Post, Detroit News, Elyria* (Ohio) *Chronicle, Eugene* (Ore.) *Register-Guard, Gulfport* (Miss.) *Herald, Idaho Statesman, Indianapolis Star,* Jack Anderson Associates, *Kansas City Star,* KGUN-TV Tucson, *Miami Herald, Milwaukee Journal, Newsday,* Reno Newspapers, *Riverside* (Calif.) *Press, St. Louis Globe-Democrat, Seers Rio Grande Weekly, Tulsa Tribune,* Urban Policy Research Institute (Calif.), *Washington Star,* and *Wenatchee* (Wash.) *World.*

The first of the Arizona Squad came to Phoenix on October 1, 1976, and a little over five months later, in early March of 1977, the twenty-three-part series on crime in Arizona was ready for publication, or so it was considered by Robert Greene, Pulitzer Prize-winning senior editor of *Newsday,* who headed up the Arizona Project.

In the period of nearly half a year, the IRE reporters spent their twelve-to-fifteen-hour working days digging into the subterranean recesses of crime in the state. Interview after interview with hundreds of informants, law-enforcement officials, politicians, and underworld characters was made. Voluminous amounts of information flowed into their files from letters, telephone calls, and personal contacts.

Investigators from the IRE roamed all over the Southwest and into Mexico, while nervous politicians and worried criminals quivered in fearful anticipation.

Rumors were rampant. Most everyone in Arizona knew the heat was on.

Finally, in early March only the writers were left, the investigations were done, and all that remained was to read the revelations in participating newspapers, see them on television, or hear them on the radio. The IRE reports were ready—or were they?

On March 13, 1977, the date set for publication of the first in the series of twenty-three articles, well-wishers were stunned. A number of the big participating newspapers, such as the *Chicago Tribune*, the *Milwaukee Journal*, the *Washington Star*, and Don Bolles' own newspaper, the *Arizona Republic*, refused to run the story as sent to them by the IRE's Arizona Squad.

Other participants ran the full story, but most either used a judiciously edited version or relied on Associated Press or United Press International wire service condensations.

Why?

It was easy to understand the lack of play from newspapers such as the *New York Times*, the *Los Angeles Times*, and the *Washington Post* which refused to participate in the project at its inception, for they had either expressed an aversion to *group journalism* or simply didn't want to print investigative stories over which they had no direct control. But the reluctance of the project participants was a shock.

The answers to "Why?" began to trickle in.

The managing editor of the *Chicago Tribune*, Maxwell McCrohon, said, "Two *Tribune* editors who have grappled with this book-sized report have concluded that it is not ready for printing in the *Tribune* in its present form."

Others voiced concern that allegations in the series, though colorful, were insufficiently documented and inadequately supported.

221

Robert Greene, head of the Arizona Squad, denied this.

City Editor Mike Murphy of the *Los Angeles Times*, when asked for comments on the IRE series, said simply, "We haven't seen anything that excites us."

But there was a lot of initial excitement in Arizona, as readers struggled to get copies of papers carrying the IRE series. Phoenicians unable to find anything in the *Republic* or *Gazette* searched frantically to find copies of the Tucson newspaper the *Arizona Star*, which was carrying edited versions of the IRE articles.

Several days after the series began, the R&G started to carry on its inside pages Associated Press stories and condensations on the IRE series. This obviously was in response to an irate readership opposed to what was in essence a virtual news blackout on the details of the IRE charges.

Some Phoenicians even set up picket lines around the R&G printing plant in protest.

In the state Legislature, Senator Sue Dye, D-Tucson, stood up and accused the R&G of not running the IRE series because "it might prove detrimental to some of their favorite sons."

Arizona's radio and television stations, however, were having a ball running whatever they could lay their hands on, and the essence of the IRE reports began to filter through, even in Phoenix.

The first article was a stage setter, a generalized overview of crime in Arizona.

It stated that the premise of the IRE team was not to investigate the Bolles murder but to carry on the reporter's work as a final tribute to him and the people he sought to inform. It also said that the promise of Arizona was being siphoned away by organized crime, corrupt political structures, and a justice system that was being crippled by evils that ranged from cronyism to flat-out dishonesty.

It suggested historic and continuing relationships between underworld chieftains and influential politicians in the state, and that the parsimonious law-enforcement budgets which forced police to concentrate on high-profile street crime and ignore other matters were the fruits of these relationships.

It also said that the state has become "perhaps the single most concentrated corridor of illegal drug entry in the U.S.," and quoted many law-enforcement officials on the insufficiency of the state's anti-crime activities.

While some of the descriptive terms used, particularly in the full-length version run by such newspapers as *Newsday*, seemed a bit exaggerated, there was little to criticize in the first article.

One sentence said, "Organized crime, dominated by such jet-age mobsters as Moe Dalitz, Joe Bonanno, and Peter Licavoli, is staging an *invasion* of Phoenix, Tucson, and other Arizona cities." The word "invasion" generally connotes something like D day in Normandy during World War II, and suggests literal masses of humanity inundating some specific place. To objective observers a word such as "infiltrate" may have been a better choice.

The first article's obvious purpose was to indicate the scope of the series, and stimulate reader interest in the articles to come. This it did, and did it well.

Then, they hit with the biggest Arizona *names* they could find, U. S. Senator Barry Goldwater and his friend, Phoenix businessman and politician Harry Rosenzweig, along with Goldwater's brother, Robert, and tied them to a host of nationally known mobsters.

"Goldwater Tied to the Mob," was the headline pitch, and despite the announced reluctance by some, the national news media ran with the ball. Goldwater was a national figure, and the story seemed juicy.

IRE articles No. 2 through No. 6 dwelt on the Goldwaters, Barry and Robert, and politically powerful Harry Rosenzweig. These articles accused them of accepting the presence of organized crime through friendships and business alliances with mob figures.

But as the stories on the senator and his boyhood chum Rosenzweig were released, an unexpected phenomenon began making the rounds in Arizona. The heat of enthusiasm for the IRE revelations began to cool.

Arizonans who had been waiting with not so patient expectation for new revelations found little in the IRE texts that was not already known and published many years ago. Material on the lesser-known Robert Goldwater brought on a few "oohs" and "ahs," but even this didn't incite an oust Goldwater movement. Apparently more had been expected, perhaps *current* ties to organized crime or alleged illegalities.

The senator, responding to the IRE allegations, branded as "completely untrue" the charges that he had condoned the presence of organized crime. Goldwater said the IRE stories relating to himself were "dishonest," and on ABC Television's "Good Morning, America" program said, "I'm shocked and I'm resentful."

Nothing criminal was charged against the Arizona senator. Even Robert Greene, who was the leader and spokesman for the IRE group, was quoted by the Associated Press as saying, "I truthfully don't think Barry Goldwater has committed a crime, but he has a thirty-year history of associating openly with some of the principal crime figures in the Phoenix area. Is this wrong? We maintain yes."

The articles did not cite any personal connection between either Barry Goldwater or Harry Rosenzweig and Arizona's best-known Mafia figure, Joe Bonanno, but said that there were relationships with mobster Willie Bioff; Gus Greenbaum, who was described as a top Meyer Lansky aide; Clarence (Mike) Newman, a Phoenix gambler; and Joseph P. Ceferatti, a former insurance broker with alleged underworld-linked business dealings.

Willie Bioff was known as a labor racketeer who was in on an organized-crime effort to take over the motion picture unions in Hollywood in the late thirties and early forties. As a result of his participation in shakedown attempts, he was caught and convicted. Then, after spending a short time in prison, he was paroled. This parole resulted from his agreement to testify in the 1943 extortion trial against Sidney Korshak, a labor lawyer with mob connections. He also testified against five members of the old Capone mob in another trial. For this testimony the U. S. government made a deal. John Bradshaw in *New York* magazine wrote, "Bioff was probably the first criminal to have taken refuge under the federal 'alias' program, and for a time most people knew him as Willie Nelson."

In this regard, the IRE report simply said, "Afterward, he moved to Phoenix under the name William Nelson to hide his gangland past." The IRE report neglected to point out what was well known in Arizona, that Willie Bioff established himself in the state under the alias "William Nelson" with the concurrence and actual assistance of the Department of Justice. This omission suggested to many that "investigative reporting" had been put aside, and the IRE was merely interested in doing a "hatchet job" on Goldwater and Rosenzweig.

Goldwater in responding to the IRE charges that Willie Bioff had contributed to one of his political campaigns said, "That is true. My wife's uncle, long since passed away, called me one day to see if I would take a check from a friend of his. I said, 'Certainly.' So he brought this man in and introduced him as Bill Nelson, and he gave a check, I think to Harry Rosenzweig. But about five weeks after the election, he came into my office with a picture I had given him and said, 'Don't you know who I am?' 'You're Bill Nelson,' I replied. Then he said, 'No, I'm Willie Bioff!' Well, I knew who Willie Bioff was . . . so he tore up the picture, and said he didn't want it found in his possession."

Goldwater said that later, he did fly Bioff and his wife back to Phoenix when Bioff's commercial flight was grounded and he met him accidentally at the airport. "Knowing that the press would get ahold of it," Goldwater commented, "I called Westbrook Pegler, long since dead, but he wrote the complete story and it appeared in the newspapers—oh, Lord! that's twenty-two years ago. So, that's Bioff!"

The same incident was also disclosed in a book, *The Green Felt Jungle.*

Bioff was murdered in November 1955 when a bomb planted in his pick-up truck exploded.

Gus Greenbaum, who came to Arizona in 1928, was first a Phoenix businessman who later ran a "race wire service" and booked horse bets in the wide-open climate of pre-1940 Arizona. In the late forties, he became manager of the Flamingo Hotel on The Strip in Las Vegas, the first of the large casino-hotels to open. In 1958, after problems with organized-crime interests in Las Vegas, he and his wife were found in their Phoenix home with their throats slit.

Another aspect of the IRE allegations which puzzled Arizonans familiar with the old Bioff and Greenbaum connections was the use of these associations to prove that Goldwater was tied in with organized crime. Both Bioff and Greenbaum were *losers,* minor figures as mobsters go, who were eliminated by the underworld. Neither of them was very popular or powerful in the crime syndicate structure. If this was the best the IRE could come up with, these Arizonans surmised, the IRE was using rather weak evidence to prove its point.

Even Democratic political foes of Republicans Goldwater and Rosenzweig were unhappy with the IRE's introductory articles.

Arizona Senator Dennis DeConcini, Democrat, was asked if he thought the IRE series took some "cheap shots," as others had contended. "I think they did, and it's too bad, because overall I think they did a service to Arizona. I don't think they needed to take all the cheap shots they did.

"Those who know the other side of some of the people they took the cheap shots at, and some of them are Republicans, made the IRE lose its credibility," DeConcini stressed, "and it's too bad, because you don't need to go into the stuff they went into that doesn't show any criminality, since all it shows is some very poor judgment on people's parts. I'm sorry they did that," he concluded, "because there's enough that they have printed that I'm satisfied is true and is bad for Arizona, without losing their credibility."

It was also reported that the state Legislature had lost interest in a Crime Task Force, a former top-priority item, due principally to a widespread opinion among legislators that the IRE series, which was expected to be a bombshell, just *bombed*, instead.

Benjamin Bradlee, executive editor of the *Washington Post*, said he disagreed with the "group journalism" concept and thought that the subject matter could best be handled by investigative reporters within the state. He had a point. Perhaps one has to be in the state for a few years before one can get the "feel" of it.

Take the old wealthy families who have been so influential in Arizona, some of whom were powers in its territorial days. Despite jets, computers, and atomic energy, they still retain the mores and psychological patterns of the frontier West.

This can be seen, particularly, in the attitudes of the older generation toward newcomers to the state. As long as the newcomer isn't a troublemaker, seems reasonably industrious, takes care of the wife and kids, and fits in with social life of the community, he is acceptable. Past reputations mean little, and as it was in the old days, they will accept a person on face value.

Among these people, there is also a fierce loyalty toward old friends and acquaintances, which manifests itself in sort of a *noblesse oblige*, a feeling of responsibility toward old friends and acquaintances that an old-time family might feel and exhibit toward one another.

Barry Goldwater, his brother, and Harry Rosenzweig were all products of this era passed. Barry and Harry in particular have a rugged, outspoken "ranch boss" quality in their personality make-up which is evident even to an interviewer. Neither chooses his words with practiced care, and both display an impulsive candor which makes it difficult to place either in the category of a Machiavellian villain.

Perhaps these personality traits also account for the differing assessment of these men by the IRE and Arizonans who have known them for a greater period of time.

By leading off the series with the past associations of Goldwater and Rosenzweig, many have suggested, the IRE gave the appearance that they were more interested in sensational stories than in uncovering current criminal activities in the state.

Put in their proper context, it is suggested, the associations of Goldwater and Rosenzweig would have been more useful, perhaps, as a demonstration of how people with criminal ties and intent can penetrate the business and social life of a still somewhat bucolic Western state.

But all is not negative from the IRE point of view.

Despite the refusals to publish, and the criticisms

228

voiced, Robert Greene of the IRE has said that the goals of the project have been achieved.

There is no doubt that an enormous amount of publicity has focused attention on Arizona and its crime problems, and perhaps in a sense this is not only a warning to criminals to lay off attacking reporters, but also a valid extension of Don Bolles' investigative work.

In addition, some Arizonans are capable of looking past the cheap-shot syndrome to the good they have found in other parts of the IRE series.

John Ahearn, Phoenix attorney, and a leading figure for many years in the Democratic party, joined in partial praise of the IRE articles.

"I thought the stuff done on the drug rings was done excellently, and I haven't seen that anywhere in the public print," he said.

He also commended the stories on Ned Warren, reputed godfather of Arizona land fraud.

"I thought that by compiling all that evidence against Warren in a two-part story, they have done us a service," Ahearn commented.

"They brought it up to date, and chronologically showed the connections with the various corporations," he continued, "and that was eye opening to me. Here I am a lawyer," he stressed in amazement, "and I never realized that he [Warren] was involved in about seventy companies."

Warren frankly admitted during an interview with IRE reporters that he was something less than a choir boy. "I was a thief—and a good thief!" he was quoted as saying.

Warren's criminal activities were originally brought to light by investigative reporter Don Bolles in 1967.

Jonathan Marshall, newspaper publisher of the award-winning *Scottsdale Daily Progress*, gave the IRE series its due when asked to comment on the status of crime in Phoenix and the state.

"Everyone knows we've got big Mafia operations," he said. "But I didn't know it was nearly as big as it is until I read the IRE report, frankly. One of the big things it [IRE series] did was to bring us some *specifics* on things like the Mafia, and how they have infiltrated the state," Marshall continued. "I knew there was a lot of dope smuggling, but I didn't know the extent of it though [until the IRE reports]."

The Associated Press gave a good capsulized description of the IRE articles:

"Accounts of the series, which runs about 100,000 words in all, present a massive collection of names, dates, and places that figure in intricate stock, land, and other business deals, mainly in Arizona and Nevada. It also details a web of social relationships linking businessmen, celebrities, sports figures, unions, and gangsters."

"For the most part," the AP description continued, "the published accounts have not alleged any new crimes. Rather, they present a picture of well-known business and political leaders dealing with people who are linked—sometimes indirectly—to organized crime."

While there are many within the state who consider the guilt by association stories on Goldwater and Rosenzweig as cheap shots, many are also willing to admit that Arizona's national-level politicians have done little in the past to alert the state to the possible infiltration by organized crime. Only former congressman Sam Steiger raised much of a ruckus over what he thought was an organized-crime inroad when he launched his campaign against the Emprise Corporation.

Senator Barry Goldwater displays at times an almost incomprehensible lack of knowledge on organized-crime activities, and demonstrates no great interest in improving that knowledge. Goldwater, responding to a question at a recent news conference if he knew that Gus Greenbaum was associated with Meyer Lansky, said, "I never heard of Meyer Lansky until I talked to Barbara Walters about twenty minutes ago—and I asked her who the man was."

Meyer Lansky is a crime syndicate celebrity who has received more publicity than almost any reputed mob figure with the possible exception of Al Capone. How Senator Goldwater could have avoided some fragmentary knowledge of Meyer Lansky seems nearly beyond the realm of possibility.

When asked at the same news conference whether he thought Arizona was infiltrated by the Mafia, Goldwater replied, "No, I don't believe it! I don't think that they [the IRE] can prove it—in fact, I defy them to prove it," he continued.

"I have known of only one man in Tucson— Bonanno or something like that—who bought a racetrack and later sold it," he said. "I have not had any indications from law officers, nor have I had any indications from *anybody* that any members of the Mafia have moved into Arizona."

This statement was also greeted by incredulous amazement, since the presence of reputed mob figures in the state has received considerable publicity over the years.

Since the early 1950s stories on reputed mobsters residing in Arizona have been appearing frequently in the Tucson press. Don Bolles and Jack West wrote an in-depth series on mobsters in the state for the *Arizona Republic*, and author Gay Talese wrote a best-selling book entitled *Honor Thy Father* which was made into a television movie. All of these told not only of Joe Bonanno, but of many other reputed mob figures entrenched in Arizona, and there were many other forms of regional and national publicity on the subject.

Yet the U. S. senator from the state of Arizona said he had no indication from anybody that the Mafia existed in the state.

Harry Rosenzweig, former chairman of the state Republican party for many years, has also voiced a similar ignorance of organized-crime activities.

"I don't know any of the *families* that are here [Phoenix]. I don't know the Bonannos and Licavolis. I know they live in Tucson, but I've never heard of anything," Rosenzweig said. "Is Bonanno still alive?" he questioned.

The apparent lack of knowledge by Goldwater and Rosenzweig indicates to a number of Arizonans an abysmal lack of concern on the subject, and demonstrates the "live and let live" attitude in which they contend the Arizona establishment is steeped.

"As long as the guy doesn't bother me, I really don't give a damn what he does," is nearly a cliché in the state, according to many critics of leadership in the state.

Perhaps the dangers inherent in this attitude were what the earlier IRE articles were attempting to point out. But it's unfortunate, many suggest, that the IRE chose a club rather than a scalpel to eliminate the problem.

People often ask, "Did the IRE series help law-enforcement agencies uncover anything new?"

The new United States Attorney for Arizona, Mike Hawkins, was interviewed on a Phoenix television station (KOOL-TV) and responded to this question by saying, "During the time the IRE investigators were here in Arizona doing their work, they were cooperative with us in the sense that they would occasionally contact our investigators and say that they had encountered a factual area that maybe we ought to take a look at.

"In many cases they had things we already were

looking at," Hawkins said, "and in some cases there were things we had not been taking a look at—and we are now in the process of several ongoing investigations that relate factually to some of the things that the IRE team uncovered.

"Whether they will lead to criminal prosecution is simply too premature at this time to comment on," he said, then stressed, "but they *are* being worked on."

In the same interview, Hawkins offered this comment: "I don't think there is any question that the focus that the IRE series has brought to Arizona makes it [his job] easier to do."

Former U. S. Attorney William Smitherman, however, was not so complimentary, as he has been quoted as saying, "I expected something more." Smitherman also stated publicly his displeasure over the use of the IRE of what he described as "old, previously published material."

Arizona Attorney General Bruce Babbitt was more eloquent in his assessment of the IRE series. "It serves the same purpose as all good journalism. It calls significant facts to the attention of the public and maintains pressure for reform. It is doing that very amply."

Continuing the quote from an AP article, Babbitt said, "The articles [IRE] have been useful to the attorney general's office, but it would be a mistake to view it primarily that way. Journalism is not a form of law enforcement."

As the name states, the IRE is an organization made up of investigative reporters and editors, and obviously their intent was to advance the cause of investigative journalism. And, as previously mentioned, the Arizona Squad was an experiment in which investigative journalism was attempted by a group of reporters and editors who were subject to few restraints other than their own.

233

As indicated, the results of this effort received mixed reviews.

What some respected members of the journalistic profession seem to suggest in their criticism of the IRE project is that any crusade by the news media, regardless of merit, cannot sustain the objectivity necessary to good journalism. And from its own statement of purpose, the IRE project was in essence a crusade against crime in Arizona, and a threat to crucify any criminal element that may take a notion to *waste* a reporter.

Even professionals with good credentials can lose their objectivity, they suggest, when zeal born of emotion and worthy purpose takes over the typewriter.

These thoughtful journalists, cognizant of their own weaknesses, say it is highly probable that this well-intentioned zeal will manifest itself in allegations which are insufficiently documented and inadequately supported. These were the very charges made against the IRE series.

In an article by Judith Frutig of *The Christian Science Monitor*, Benjamin Bradlee, executive editor of the *Washington Post*, was quoted on his opinion that the IRE series lacked sufficient documentation.

"My favorite paragraph [in Part 3 of the series]," said Mr. Bradlee, "says police also have overheard a complaint by Joseph [Papa Joe] Tocco, [former] operator of a restaurant that serves as a post office for Chicago crime syndicate transplants, that Rosenzweig and other businessmen had prostitution so locked up that the Cosa Nostra could get only a small bit of the action. Here you have an anonymous police officer quoting an unnamed informant who overheard an unspecified complaint in a restaurant by a crook. You can't get away with that . . ." Bradlee declared.

Anthony Insolia, managing editor of *Newsday* and story editor for the Arizona Project, defended the series by saying, "It's very easy for Mr. Bradlee to sit back and criticize the vagueness of the way it came out in print. To assume it was not backed up by sufficient documentation is rather arrogant."

One way to measure the accuracy and documentation of an investigative story is to count the ensuing legal actions.

While a number of persons mentioned in the IRE articles have said they were contemplating legal action, only five, as of this writing, have actually filed suit. Among them are: Peter Licavoli, Jr., son of reputed mobster Peter Licavoli, who the IRE said was running a crime syndicate operation that included drugs and prostitution; Alfred Gay, the owner of a small border town, whom the IRE series has called "the mystery man of the border"; and Phoenix Suns general manager Jerry Colangelo, who IRE suggested was a frequenter of places known to be gamblers' hangouts.

The best measurement, however, of the IRE effort must be the impact it has had on the state for better or worse.

One evaluation by a concerned Phoenix attorney, John Ahearn, no doubt expresses the view of one sizable segment of the Arizona scene.

He said, "I had hoped that it [the series] would show in a wrap-up the relationships between the politicians, business, and the Mafia. But this was never done! It was kind of a chronological story without any warp or woof to it—and I was disappointed in that regard.

"But the series did us a good service," he remarked. I'll concede shoddy writing, I'll concede lousy editing, and I'll concede some of it as rehash," Ahearn continued, "but I will not concede the major points made by the series."

It is evident, however, from the lack of discernible outrage and impetus for action that most people were so *turned off* by what they deemed unfair innuendo and associations in the first few articles that the whole series suffered a loss of credibility.

Robert Greene, leader of the IRE project, was quoted in AP as telling an awards audience in Chicago that any reforms resulting from the series depend on "the government and the people of Arizona. Our job was to present the information," he said, "but unless there is a huge public outcry, nothing will happen."

Nothing much *has* happened!

Unfortunately, it appears that a good, well-intentioned project was trapped by its own zealous efforts and the by-products of advocacy journalism.

More unfortunate still is the high probability that these noble efforts may cause true investigative journalism in Arizona to join Don Bolles in the lonely quiet of a desert graveyard.

Aftermath

ARIZONA, U.S.A.

On June 2, 1976, Don Bolles, an investigative reporter, was blasted to shreds at a hotel parking lot in Phoenix. This brutal incident has become a directional signpost for the leadership in the state of Arizona. The direction they take will determine the destiny of the state for many years to come.

Will Arizona be a concerned, vigorous example of a clean, healthy United States or will it be a crime-ridden "Disneyland" demonstrating the worst traits of the American character and economic system? The choice is up to its leadership.

Arizonans may not realize it, but many people around the world are watching the events in this state as an indicator of the U.S. resolve in the area of human rights. Can Arizona clean up its own mess, or will it be business as usual with a lip-service veneer?

Many in the world community are asking if Americans are really interested in defending the rights of the average person from oppressive evils, or are they just wrapped up in making the fast buck. Arizona's approach to its crime problem could furnish an answer.

Like Watergate, the bombing murder of Don Bolles has become a *cause célèbre*. Many view it as a slap in the face, a challenge by organized criminals to a political and economic system based on ethics and morality.

In life, Don Bolles was a pleasant better-than-average investigative journalist who loved his wife and kids, made some mistakes as we all do, and played a constructive role in the community.

In death, however, he has become something else.

Amplified by circumstance and situation, the Bolles image has expanded into a pervading specter of conscience that continues to permeate the state, the nation, and the profession to which he belonged.

Deep down, in the journalistic innards of every legitimate member of the news-gathering profession, the murder of Don Bolles has left its mark.

To some who ply his trade, Bolles' murder has strengthened the resolve to dig deeper and ferret out more of the unpleasant facts and hidden truths about crime in America.

To others, it has simply strengthened their natural cynicism. These cynics say that the public at large doesn't really give a damn, that it secretly admires the successful big-time criminal as long as his activity doesn't affect them as individuals. There may be some truth in this cynicism, but is it the public's fault?

In most societies, crusaders are few and far between. The overwhelming majority whether journalist or average citizen follow the trends established by their leaders or bosses. If this contention is true, as seems evident, then the blame for the criminal activity in the state rests squarely in the laps of Arizona's political, social, and economic leaders.

The usual cop-out by entrepreneurs in business and politics is that they give the people what they want. It is the free market or the will of the electorate that determines the course of action, they say. Nonsense! Since when have the people demanded inflationary prices, unemployment, a polluted land, or a rising crime rate?

Actually, the focus on Arizona resulting from the

Bolles murder and the IRE reports has stimulated some anti-crime activity, but much of it is more cosmetic in nature than significant.

The greatest strides have been made in the prosecution of the more obvious types of land fraud. Cochise College Park, a land company controlled by Ned Warren, reputed godfather of land fraud, was brought into federal court and six persons were convicted of bilking more than ten thousand investors out of some $37 million. Each of the defendants was found guilty of thirty-three counts of mail fraud, securities fraud, and interstate transportation of money obtained by fraud.

United States Attorney for Arizona Mike Hawkins says, "There's more to come."

There have also been a number of convictions at the state and county level.

The state Real Estate Department appears alert and eager under Commissioner George Snyder, and the state Land Department is in equally good shape with a concerned and ethics-oriented lawyer, Andrew Bettwy, Sr., at its helm.

However, it is still legal for the state of Arizona to sell "school trust lands" in any amount to private interests by "labeling" it as commercial land, and a request by Land Commissioner Bettwy to look into the Lake Havasu situation has not as yet brought a response from the attorney general's office.

All in all, the phrase "caveat emptor" has not as yet been removed from the state's escutcheon.

In the state Legislature, some members of the House and Senate Judiciary committees are receiving praise for pushing through the first revision of the state's Criminal Codes since 1912 when Arizona joined the Union.

After a three-year study by a select commission of interested citizens and members of the legal community, the proposed Criminal Code was ripped apart and reassembled by the Legislature's Judiciary committees, and sent to the floors of the respective houses for passage. It has removed from the statute books such crimes as the destruction of birds' nests in cemeteries, and decreased the penalty for adultery, open and notorious cohabitation, and consensual conduct among adults from a felony to a misdemeanor.

Basically, the new Code reorganizes and clarifies existing law, but it also adds the politically appealing mandatory sentences for violent street crimes.

It classifies all crimes to six classes of felonies, three classes of misdemeanors, and one group called "petty offenses." There are presumptive sentences fixed to each category of felony, a device by which widely varying sentences for the same crime are expected to be controlled.

Other major changes are in the areas of parole, probation, and the restoration of civil rights.

This revision of the Criminal Code is a lengthy document, long overdue, which updates Arizona's "Billy the Kid" laws in the genre of violent or poor man's crimes, but for some inexplicable reason seems to do little in the areas involving organized or white collar crime.

Though the revised Code adopts stronger measures to deal with loansharking and fencing, it was reported that the Legislature's joint conference committee was *unable to agree* on a proposal which would give the attorney general a truly effective weapon against organized crime, the state RICO measure.

This was a proposal patterned after the federal Racketeer-Influenced and Corrupt Organizations statute which makes it a crime to use illegally obtained money to fund legitimate businesses.

The proposal, it is also reported, would have given broad search and seizure powers to the attorney general of the state.

It seems that big money, regardless of its origin, is the earwax that prevents legislators from hearing the will of the people. Of all the measures in the revised Code, the one which could have had the greatest impact on big-time criminals was dropped.

Why?

Another "Max Factor" measure was the establishment of the joint legislative Crime Task Force.

Prior to publication of the IRE reports, when the reporters were digging into Arizona's dirt, a nervous Legislature, to show its interest in cleaning up the state, approved this Crime Task Force, which like the investigative committees in Washington would dig into the state's organized-crime activities and their relationship with state agencies. They hired ex-U.S. attorney William Smitherman, a Republican, to head up the group, and growled menacingly at the mafiosi and white collar crooks who reside in the state.

But when the IRE reports were received in the state with somewhat less than overwhelming enthusiasm, the Arizona legislators seemed to lose their zeal to battle the mobsters and discovered that party politics could be lurking in this investigative vehicle.

Democrats began to say that the Republican-controlled House of Representatives was going to make political capital out of the hearings that would ensue, and that the whole idea was just a gimmick to push Republican Bill Smitherman for some future state political office.

Republicans wryly suggested that Democrat Dennis DeConcini had made a name for himself by being appointed to the four-county Drug Strike Force by Democrat Governor Raul Castro, so why the "holler"?

With the IRE pressure gone, and the R&G newspaper monopoly less than "ape" over the task force, Senate Democrats launched a campaign to "depoliticize" the Crime Task Force by emasculating its power to grant immunity to witnesses.

Senate Majority Leader Alfredo Gutierrez reportedly said, "We don't need a legislative police force."

Senator Frank Felix of Tucson, a Democrat, commented in a published report, "We're doing a public relations job for the Legislature to the tune of $464,000. That money," he reportedly said, "could be better spent if we gave it to the attorney general or county attorneys, who have the facilities and expertise in these areas."

An amendment similar to the final one which made the strike force impotent was rejected earlier when Smitherman testified that it would make it impossible for the task force to investigate shady corporations. Without immunity, he contended, a lot of these people won't "talk."

Perhaps this *is* just a launching pad for Smitherman's political ambitions, and perhaps the Republicans are looking for a forum to demonstrate to the voters that they too are interested in fighting organized crime, but there is another, more sinister aspect to the castration of the task force. This is the fact that such a task force is about the only way the inroads of organized crime can be brought to the attention of the people of Arizona.

Legal prosecution by its very nature confines testimony to a generally narrow avenue of inquiry as outlined by the charges. There is insufficient latitude to probe into such things as general practices, unethical dealings, or a multiplicity of criminal activities. Only through public hearings on the nature, extent, and structure of organized crime can its operations be revealed, and an investigatory body such as the Crime Task Force is necessary to determine whether government itself is consciously or unconsciously aiding criminals through its laws and policies.

Public hearings by a legislative committee, aided by the investigative staff of a Crime Task Force, would demand news coverage by the state's news media, including the R&G newspaper monopoly, and for political considerations if nothing else, the hearings would have to come up with substantive investigative material on organized crime and its relationships with the state government.

On June 2, 1977, exactly one year after Don Bolles was bombed, Governor Raul Castro vetoed the *joint* task force.

A number of state representatives say an emasculated version may be revived in the next legislative session as strictly a House-supported Crime Task Force with no state Senate participation. Local political pundits suggest such an action could prove beneficial to the Republican party in the state, and provide it with a media platform for the upcoming gubernatorial election. The House as previously mentioned is controlled by the Republicans.

Meanwhile, crime-fighting has taken a back seat in other sections of the political arena.

With Governor Raul Castro fading from favor with his own party due to patronage problems and an oratorical ineptitude, the leadership of the Democratic party is splitting into two basic camps who will be fighting for control. These are the factions who look to the tall, blond, bespectacled image of Attorney General Bruce Babbitt and Tucson's crime-fighting champion, U. S. Senator Dennis DeConcini, for party direction.

The split between the Babbitt and DeConcini factions could weaken the Democrats as a political power in the state, and cause a complete halt in any effective anti-crime effort.

Babbitt, a consummate politician, projects the public image of a humble, earnest, and sincere young attorney who works tirelessly at the job of being a good attor-

243

ney general at a very bad time. He is very popular with the press, comes across on television like a fledgling Estes Kefauver, and looks like the number-one contender for governor.

Originally a "tiger" when he demanded and got a state-wide grand jury, and later when he took the Bolles case away from the Maricopa county attorney, Babbitt in recent months has mellowed considerably.

In recent months he has had a tendency to play it safe in discussing controversial matters with the news media, and while saying that organized and white collar crime continues to exist, he has joined the R&G monopoly in offering such platitudes as "things are getting better" and "we're making progress."

Secretive on what, if any, progress is being made in the prosecution of organized or white collar criminals, he has many critics in the law-enforcement field who ask, "What has he done?"

When asked for his assessment of Mafia activities in the state during a recent interview, Babbitt said, "I think it's too early to tell—I don't think there is any way to tell at this point."

When queried about organized crime's penetration of Arizona business, he replied, "There's some evidence of that. I don't think anybody knows how far it goes."

The other powerful Democratic figure who has acquired a dominant position in the party, U. S. Senator Dennis DeConcini, criticizes crime in the state but apparently has no wish to lead a crusade to eradicate it. As a freshman U. S. senator, DeConcini is somewhat limited by his involvement in a crash course to learn the Washington ropes. Like Babbitt, however, he appears to have joined the establishment in the "cool it" campaign.

While he has placed a campaign aide, Mike Hawkins, in the U. S. Attorney's office in Phoenix, and applied some pressure on the Justice Department to beef up its personnel and facilities in the area, most state political activity has been placed in the hands of his brother, Dino DeConcini, the current executive assistant to Governor Raul Castro. Dino, it is said, may be an opponent for Bruce Babbitt in the next Democratic gubernatorial primary.

On the other side of the Arizona political fence, William Smitherman, the Republican crime-fighting hero and possible candidate for attorney general or governor, is casting his lot with the Republican-controlled House of Representatives to provide himself with the tools for recognition and political advancement.

Not the foremost proponent of humility and self-effacement in the state of Arizona, Smitherman considers himself the state's foremost prosecutor of white collar criminals.

"I'm the only son of a bitch around here who's ever done anything about organized crime, or white collar crime, or anything else of any magnitude," he shyly expressed during an interview.

While Smitherman may be inordinately impressed with himself, no one in Arizona has yet had the temerity to suggest that this former U. S. Attorney is a desert copy of Sir Galahad or Tom Dewey.

Not exactly a fan of the current attorney general, Bruce Babbitt, he responded to an interview question on whether state money for his Crime Task Force would be more effectively spent if allocated to the AG's office by retorting, "The attorney general hasn't put anybody in jail that I know about—do you know of any?"

Meanwhile, the top police official in state government, Department of Public Safety Director Vernon Hoy, raised a lot of legislative hackles by suggesting that the Appropriations Committee of the Arizona state Senate was "rotten with politics," and its crime-fighting efforts were mere "window dressing."

Hoy's attacks stemmed from the Appropriations Committee's action which slashed the state police budget in half.

Vernon Hoy is an ex-Los Angeles Police Department official who was brought in from California several years ago to renovate Arizona's state law-enforcement agency.

The old and entrenched DPS hierarchy had acquired a reputation more for their proclivity to build departmental "empires" than for an outstanding ability to fight crime. Hoy revealed that when he came "on board," he was offered a slush fund by the Association of Highway Patrolmen to help defray expenses of various sorts, including those which might be expended to keep legislators happy with the DPS operation. In Hoy's view, the existence of such a slush fund was wrong, though its use was common gossip prior to his arrival on the scene.

In the eyes of some, Hoy's puritanical attitude and his dismissal of some of the "good ole boys" from the previous administration were not playing the game. As a result, Hoy created legislative enemies who were more at ease with the old politically discerning DPS officials than with Hoy's "straight arrow" approach.

The pragmatic effect of these efforts to clean house and establish a truly professional department was the budgetary knife for requested allocations.

In addition to arousing Vernon Hoy's personal ire, the chopping in half of the requested budget has caused a lowering of the department's morale, and increased the feeling among state law-enforcement personnel that they are underpaid and underappreciated by Arizona's lawmakers.

An investigation that grew out of Hoy's charges against the state Senate indicates that there has been no provable use of the AHP slush fund to butter up the Legislature in the recent past, but the legislative furor caused by Hoy's charges and the Senate's niggardly approach to anti-crime funding have done little to assure Arizonans that a war against crime exists in the state.

On the county level, new prosecutorial blood in some of the county attorney's offices has produced healthier and positive results.

In Pima County (Tucson), County Attorney Steve Neeley is reported to be working effectively with the four-county Drug Traffic Strike Force.

According to Senator DeConcini, Neeley is also working on an informal research project which takes a look at anti-organized-crime and pro-law-enforcement legislation which has been introduced in the state Legislature in the past, but killed in committee or on the floor before it's seen the light of day.

DeConcini says Neeley wants to see how much neglect there has been, and whether there has been any conspiracy to prevent law-enforcement legislation from passing.

In Maricopa County, County Attorney Charles Hyder has not been timid in requesting additional funds.

At a public hearing, Hyder told the Maricopa County board of supervisors that he needed a budget increase of over 50 per cent—and even if they granted the full increase it still would not be adequate. Hyder said that the Maricopa county attorney's office is so understaffed that it is literally impossible to generate investigations of governmental and police corruption.

The board of supervisors apparently has not agreed with Hyder's assessment of the situation, for the requested allocation of funds has not been forthcoming.

Meanwhile, the young county attorney has cleverly resolved the long-standing charges against the godfather of Arizona land fraud, Ned Warren, Sr.

Hyder got Warren to plead guilty to twenty-two felony counts in return for letting the ailing Warren remain in custody at his Phoenix home until sentencing. Warren, who recently underwent heart bypass surgery in Oklahoma, is described as a man in very poor health.

Trying to nail the elusive Ned Warren has been one of Charles Hyder's top-priority projects since he took office in January of 1977.

The city of Phoenix meanwhile has apparently recognized the efforts of its widely acclaimed Police Department, and particularly the highly professional work of its investigative and intelligence bureaus.

Almost alone in the state, the Phoenix Police Department has done a remarkable job of looking into the highly complex facets of white collar crime.

At a recent Exchange Club luncheon honoring Detective Lonzo McCracken, who initiated the first major investigation of a crooked land fraud operation, Phoenix Police Chief Lawrence Wetzel described the white collar criminals of the state as "apparently decent, law-abiding, church-going businessmen who become violent when their real life is exposed." He also said, "The spotlight fell on Arizona because he [McCracken] had the courage to do something about it."

Chief Wetzel added, "Everybody thought these things were civil matters, but they were just a form of stealing."

As a result of the Phoenix Police Department's effective work, Phoenix Mayor Margaret Hance has requested a doubling of the department's Organized Crime Bureau budget. Currently the budget is approximately $200,000.

Unfortunately, as fine as individual organizations may be, the attack on organized crime is unorganized. It lacks the coordinated effort between law-en-

forcement agencies and various governmental departments to make the attack meaningful and effective.
Jurisdictional disputes, departmental and interdepart-
mental jealousies, lack of adequate funding and personnel, and the quest for job security all play a part in the
feeble efforts to root out organized and white collar
crime.

Just as unfortunate is the fact that public interest in
public matters is sporadic and emotional. This is
natural perhaps.

But as time passes, a feeling of weariness and bore-
dom sets in, and the shocking atrocity of the moment is
relegated to the relative unimportance of emotional history.

As a new and impatient community, the leadership
and population of Arizona are composed mainly of
public-spirited "sprinters," and the distance runners are
but a handful.

In the Bolles case as well as other crimes, it is this
phenomenon of fading interest upon which the criminal
elements of the state depend for their survival. They
know that when resolve becomes lip service they can
once again resume their nefarious practices. It's just a
matter of keeping a low profile until the heat is off.

Tragically, powerful elements of the Arizona establishment, the so-called "good people" of the community, are unconsciously aiding and abetting these
criminals in this cooling-off process.

The *Phoenix Gazette* in a recent editorial discussing
suggested attitudes toward Arizona's bad reputation for
criminal activity said, "Arizonans should be concerned
about problems, of course, because solutions develop
out of concern. No purpose is served, however, by Arizonans having a lower opinion of conditions here than
Wall Street does [Referring to high ratings for Phoenix airport revenue bonds]. At least a look at the

bright side now and then would help a lot," the *Gazette* editorial said.

While there is nothing intrinsically wrong with this view, it does indicate the tack away from the aggressive anti-crime position of the *Republic* and *Gazette* when less than a year ago this newspaper monopoly called for "a continuing fight to wipe out for all time the criminal elements which debase and terrify this community."

The R&G is not the sole news media culprit in spreading the "Pollyanna pitch." Other sunshine crime-fighters would like to retreat to that crime-less playground where troubles melt like lemon drops.

Television stations, for example, have in recent months spent more time and money dressing up their newscasts than they have on investigating the status of organized crime in the state. The "keep off the grass" editorials presented by the Phoenix stations in particular are considered a joke. Rather than lose a listener or two, or offend some client or advertising agency, they studiously avoid attacking anything that might attack back, or so it seems.

The larger television stations in the state's major markets could well afford to fund and staff investigative projects that would be meaningful and penetrating, yet most investigative reporting is left to the *Republic* and *Gazette* in Phoenix or the *Arizona Star*. Instead, the TV outlets hire consulting organizations who come up with "show biz" formats, pretty faces, and a sensation-alized approach to graphic but superficial news.

Dead bodies, sex murderers, fires, and the weeping victims of some tragedy or other are the featured items of the standard television newscast. Apparently cater-ing to simplistic emotions and voyeurism is more profitable than generating imaginative presentations of important stories of a less emotional nature.

In addition, among the state's news media there has

been considerable criticism of the IRE reports on crime in Arizona, some of which may be justified.

However, the Arizona news media, collectively or individually, have yet to come up with a more revealing and substantial alternative. There is a general consensus that if the news media in Arizona wish to strengthen their public credibility, they must find some way to increase their durability and stamina in the presentation of important continuing stories. The war against crime, for example, is not a single emotional "charge up San Juan Hill," it is a continuing war of attrition.

The management of the state's news media monopolies must be able to summon up the courage to fight off the inroads of ennui and accusations of harping if they are to be effective in their informative campaigns for a better community.

Perhaps a disheartened Don Bolles was correct when he told former congressman Sam Steiger that it was no use to expose *anything* " 'cause nobody cares." Yet it is doubtful that Bolles, deep down, believed it himself. Don was too interested as a person and as a reporter in the world around him to surrender Arizona to the robber barons and Al Capones of today without a fight. He knew the evils and the dangers he faced, even the potential of physical harm. Some of his colleagues in the news profession teased him from time to time for checking under the hood of his car. But unlike many of us shallower members of the journalistic trade, he was aware of its hazards while doing his job.

If Bolles had a major failing, and many would consider it a virtue, he held a passionate hatred—a hatred for mobsters and crooked politicians.

It is easy to see why!

The cost of crime to the average citizen is immense.

A deputy U.S. attorney general, Joel Sacks, remarked in an interview that the money taken in white collar and organized crime, through price-fixing, extortion, theft, etc., amounts to something in the excess of a *billion dollars a month.*

"Yes, it's an incredible figure," Sacks exclaimed.

He continued, saying that if the losses from criminal activity were halted, "You could damn near wipe out our national deficit!"

The point he was making quite effectively was that crime in the United States is not something to make entertaining headlines or furnish plot material for television detective shows, it is a terrifying and enervating problem that requires strenuous and continuing efforts to combat it. The fantastic cost of crime is reflected in taxes, insurance premiums, and the cost of food, clothing, and many other necessities of life. This is why, he suggested, the war against white collar and organized crime in Arizona and elsewhere cannot be allowed to wane. It's just too damned important!

What can be done in Arizona?

From an informal survey of leaders and average citizens in the state, the following list of starter suggestions has been compiled:

1. Apply whatever pressure is necessary to force reluctant members of the state Legislature and county boards of supervisors to fund law-enforcement and prosecutorial agencies properly.

2. Demand a reassessment by the legal profession of its methods in handling unethical lawyers, and find truly effective methods to rid the profession of lawyers who aid white collar and organized criminals in the perpetration of their schemes.

3. Amend the state constitution to create a unicameral Legislature with salaries of at least $20,000 per annum and terms limited to six years.

4. Prohibit the state attorney general or county at-

torneys from running for political office for at least six years after completion of their terms of office.

5. Make the sentence for a felony committed by a public official in connection with the duties of the office a mandatory ten years in prison, with no parole.

6. Make public the ownership and tax-required financial data of all corporations incorporated within the state and computerize this information for easy access.

7. Prohibit anyone who has been convicted of corporate fraud from holding office or controlling ownership in any subsequent corporation in the state.

8. Make all corporate officers and major stockholders liable as individuals for corporate bankruptcies to 50 per cent of an individual's net worth.

9. Eliminate privately controlled title companies and institute the Torrens system of recording land titles and ownership with the state.

10. Make *all* parties involved in land sales liable for frauds they may have perpetrated in the sale.

11. Demand that the Legislature change its rules so that all votes cast by legislators in committee or on the floor will be by roll-call voting, and all such votes will be published on a daily basis during the session.

12. Publish daily reports identifying the lobbyists appearing before legislative bodies or individual legislators and for whom they are lobbying.

13. Establish a joint legislative Crime Task Force under an appropriate committee with the necessary powers of subpoena and witness immunity to make it an effective investigatory tool. In addition, prohibit any legislator or task force staff member from running for public office for a period of four years serving the elected term of office or having left the employment of the committee.

14. Through federal or state legislation (anti-trust) prohibit any one individual or corporation from owning

more than one newspaper (morning or afternoon—not both), or any other news medium within a single city.

15. Sever the connection between the State Bar Association and the State Supreme Court.

These are but a few of the suggestions offered, but they do present a starting point.

Many of these suggestions could prove beneficial in other states of the union, if adapted to the local conditions.

Very often we, as individuals, arrive at the erroneous conclusion that we have no control over the destiny of our state and nation. Despite the complexities of this day and age, it's just not true.

To justify this contention, it was mentioned earlier in this book that the Arizona state Senate had turned down an anti-crime measure which would require the annual filing of corporate financial statements and would make the willful destruction or alteration of corporate records a felony. Well, there is a postscript.

Due to Bernie Wynn's column in the *Arizona Republic*, the reaction of some concerned members of the Legislature, and some lobbying pressure by average people with no personal ax to grind, this anti-crime measure was resurrected and tacked on to a Senate-passed bill in the state House of Representatives by Representative Jim Skelly, and sent back to the Senate. This time the people's lobby drowned out the voice of private pressure, and the very same Senate that had turned the bill down before passed the measure without one single dissenting vote.

All that was necessary to accomplish this change of view was for a few interested Arizonans to get up off their comfortable "butts" and make their opinions known.

The organized criminal is still happy in his Arizona home, but he can be dispossessed if the effort is made.

The tragic death of reporter Don Bolles was the cold

water splashed in our face to wake us up. We can't go back to bed—we've got work to do!

Harry Truman was wrong, the buck doesn't stop at the presidential desk, it stops right in front of each and every one of us.

"No man is an island, entire of itself," said the poet John Donne. Each man is involved in all mankind. You *are* your brother's keeper!

All Time Bestsellers

- ☐ THE AELIAN FRAGMENT—
  George Bartram   08587-8   1.95
- ☐ THE BERLIN CONNECTION—
  Johannes Mario Simmel   08607-6   1.95
- ☐ THE BEST PEOPLE—Helen Van Slyke   08456-1   1.75
- ☐ A BRIDGE TOO FAR—Cornelius Ryan   08373-5   1.95
- ☐ THE CAESAR CODE—
  Johannes M. Simmel   08413-8   1.95
- ☐ THE CAIN CONSPIRACY—
  Johannes Mario Simmel   08535-5   1.95
- ☐ DO BLACK PATENT LEATHER SHOES
  REALLY REFLECT UP?—John R. Powers   08490-1   1.75
- ☐ THE HAB THEORY—Allen W. Eckerty   08597-5   2.50
- ☐ THE HEART LISTENS—Helen Van Slyke   08520-7   1.95
- ☐ TO KILL A MOCKINGBIRD—Harper Lee   08376-X   1.50
- ☐ THE LAST BATTLE—Cornelius Ryan   08381-6   1.95
- ☐ THE LAST CATHOLIC IN AMERICA—
  J. R. Powers   08528-2   1.50
- ☐ THE LONGEST DAY—Cornelius Ryan   08380-8   1.75
- ☐ THE MIXED BLESSING—Helen Van Slyke   08491-X   1.95
- ☐ THE MONTE CRISTO COVER UP
  Johannes Mario Simmel   08563-0   1.95
- ☐ MORWENNA—Anne Goring   08604-1   1.95
- ☐ THE RICH AND THE RIGHTEOUS
  Helen Van Slyke   08585-1   1.95
- ☐ WEBSTER'S NEW WORLD
  DICTIONARY OF THE AMERICAN
  LANGUAGE   08500-2   1.75
- ☐ WEBSTER'S NEW WORLD THESAURUS   08385-9   1.50
- ☐ THE WORLD BOOK OF HOUSE
  PLANTS—E. McDonald   03152-2   1.50

Buy them at your local bookstores or use this handy coupon for ordering:
